Jennifer Page is a freelance  *Freedom from Loneliness* is he many well-known televisio *and Earth* and *Songs of Praise. Planner,* is available from Amazon (published under her married name of Jenny Hopkin). She also writes several blogs including:

> All-The-Lonely-People.org.uk
> Inspire-Me.org.uk
> Soul2Soul.org.uk

Jennifer lives in West Yorkshire with her best friend. Her latest passion is her project Help100, in which she is trying to help 100 people in a life-changing way. All the proceeds from this book will be given to Help100 or, for sales in the USA, to the charity Five Talents.

Praise for *Freedom from Loneliness*

"a brave telling of a personal battle with loneliness…her honesty is searing and will resonate with anyone that has suffered from loneliness"

"a positive and practical guide to living a more fulfilled life whether you have feelings of loneliness or not…an enjoyable read with lots of tried and tested ideas about making the most out of life."

"I firmly believe this beautiful book will provide understanding and hope. Ms. Page also uses a bit of humour to sweeten a difficult subject matter."

"A terrific, accessible, easily digestible read, which will reassure you that you're not alone when you encounter the demon of loneliness. This book will guide you out of the maze of despair through a series of practical steps, helping you to physically, emotionally and spiritually re-connect!"

FREEDOM FROM LONELINESS

52 Ways To Stop Feeling Lonely

Jennifer Page

Dedicated to my wonderful parents and sister,
and to those fantastic friends who have helped me
when I've been feeling lonely:
Robert, Janis, Sharon, Michelle, Alison,
Mark, Steve, Clare and Nigel

With grateful thanks to Melissa for her support
and proof-reading

Contents

Foreword

It was fairly early on in the twenty five years I've spent presenting BBC Television's Songs of Praise that I realised just how much loneliness there is in the world today.

That fact hit me with real poignancy from many of the letters sent in by viewers week after week. Songs of Praise is a wonderful act of fellowship which millions of people around the world have enjoyed on Sunday evenings for the past fifty years. It is an involving mix of much-loved hymns interspersed with the stories of people who have gone through challenging experiences, and who are generous and brave enough to share the lessons they've learned along the way with others watching at home. For many of those viewers, Songs of Praise is their church and ever since we put the hymn words up on the bottom of the screen, we just know that people all over the country are singing along!

Perhaps it is that sense of togetherness and belonging that comes from hymn-singing which is one of the greatest appeals of the programme. Certainly that's what I picked up from many of the letters I received, but what was also evident was that viewers had a real sense of connection and empathy with those who spoke between the hymns. Their situations and circumstances may be very different, but what viewers identified with was their feelings. And as I read on, I realised that for so many of these letter-writers, no one ever asked them about their feelings at all! Some were married or living within families. Others lived alone through circumstance or choice. Some were widowed or divorced. There were men and women, young and old - those who were elderly, others who were younger, busy, working people. Some struggled with physical or mental health problems, whilst others found social gatherings a challenge. Some came across as capable, organised and very together in comparison to others who were still searching for a meaningful purpose in their lives. Whoever and however they were, I found myself reading between the lines of their letters to identify a chronic underlying condition: loneliness.

Isn't it odd that in this day and age when technology has enabled communication to be faster and easier than it ever has been, it is our human condition to be lonely? I believe it affects us all – perhaps not all the time, but certainly in episodes throughout our lives. You can feel loneliest of all when you're surrounded by people. You can feel achingly lonely in a marriage where the two partners find themselves simply on parallel paths, never touching, no longer needing one another. The outside world can seem fearful and frightening – but the sense that you are all alone can bring a different sort of fear, that perhaps no one will ever break through your lonely shell – or, worst still, that no one will ever want to. Loneliness makes you question your worth, your appearance, your character, your whole being. It exhausts you so that sleep is a blessed release, and yet it haunts your dreams so that you meet the dawn having slept, but not rested. It saps your confidence and ties your tongue. I remember one friend saying that she spent so many long hours alone that she felt she'd lost the art of small talk. She felt she had nothing to say that would be of interest to anyone else, so even when the opportunity of having company presented itself, she would make excuses and withdraw into her lonely shell.

You can respond to loneliness, however it strikes you, in one of two ways. You can either be reactive, so that you just accept that being lonely is your lot and adjust to that sort of life, or loneliness can challenge you to become proactive. In other words, you have a choice. Your world of experience can become diminished by your lack of what you feel is meaningful interaction with others or you can regard your lonely condition as a challenge that you want to make use of: to learn about yourself; to understand how outside influences, both people and experience, affect your peace of mind and attitude; and to recognise what you really want in terms of other people in your life.

I think people recognise in us a body language which we may not appreciate ourselves. There are times in life when, because of past hurts or current insecurities, we pull up the shutters and make it clear to others that we are not approachable. Behind those shutters, we might be feeling achingly lonely, but because our body language is uninviting, even forbidding, others give us a wide berth.

So, to be proactive in response to loneliness, to open up new possibilities and widen our daily experiences to allow others in, we have to let them know that their presence in our lives is welcome. There's an old saying that 'friendly people have friends', and there is certainly some truth in that. There is another saying that I have often lectured myself with at times when I've been brought low by loneliness: 'if you want to change your life, you have got to change your life.' Nobody can do that for you. Nobody can make you happy. Happiness is not just a condition: more often it's a decision you make for yourself. Allow yourself to be happy. Allow others to play their part. Understand that you are not always going to like everyone, anymore than everyone will like you. Recognise that sometimes being alone can bring real contentment: time to be yourself with only your own needs, interests and choices to consider.

If you met Jennifer Page, you'd see a woman who is striking to look at, creative and highly intelligent, successful, entertaining, challenging and great company. You'd never think is that someone like her could be lonely, and yet in this book she reveals her own experience in a way which will ring echoes in all of us in different ways. Her response has been proactive. She's looked the challenge of loneliness in the face, learned about herself through it, and finally reached a plateau of understanding, acceptance and justified pride in all she actually is. If that's loneliness, it seems like a pretty nice place to be.

Pam Rhodes
Presenter of BBC *Songs of Praise*

Introduction

Five out of ten of the people who (live alone) can't help themselves, and at least three of the others are irritatingly selfish. But the chances are that at some time in your life, possibly only now and then between husbands, you will find yourself settling down to a solitary existence.
~ Marjorie Hillis, *Live Alone and Like It*

I would like to think that I am between husbands at the moment, but I seem to have been between them for a very long time.

It feels strangely appropriate that I am putting the finishing touches to this book on Valentine's Day, a day on which, in recent years at least, I have felt particularly lonely and excluded from the world of love and happy coupledom that both surrounds me and eludes me. I doubt that any flowers will be unexpectedly delivered to my door today – in fact, I won't get so much as a card. And this evening, I won't be whisked off to some candlelit restaurant. I'll be sitting on my sofa, as I am now, all alone, double-checking these pages.

I have suffered from loneliness my entire life, but recently, it's started to get easier. That is not to say that I never feel lonely any more. It comes into my life sometimes and but I've learnt to deal with it, to cope with it and I'm not worrying about it so much any more.

According to the website of the mental health charity MIND, "The roots of profound loneliness may come from having been unloved as a child, so that, as an adult, they continue to feel abandoned and unlovable in all relationships, including the relationship with themselves."

That description doesn't fit me. I *was* loved as a child. I didn't feel abandoned by my parents so that doesn't explain where my loneliness comes from. Apparently people with a disability or mental illness, people who are from an ethnic minority and feel discriminated against, and people who are older, a single parent or a carer for someone disabled are all more likely to feel lonely. But I fit none of those descriptions either. I simply haven't felt like I fitted in.

Looking back over my life, I see so many moments of loneliness. Being an only child with no-one to play with. The arrival of my sister when I was 14 meaning I was no longer centre of attention. School days when I fell out with my best – and only – friend leaving me wandering the playground alone at playtimes and sitting in the school dining room by myself. Not fitting in at university because I wanted to study and my peers just seemed to want to party. Lonely times in my twenties when I split from a boyfriend and was left sitting alone in an empty flat with no-one to talk to and very little social life of my own. Lonely times in my thirties when getting married hadn't done what I had thought it would - it hadn't been the guaranteed end to loneliness that I'd imagined. In fact, being married to someone I didn't fully connect with had made my loneliness much, much worse.

So, in my mid-thirties, I got divorced. I assumed that I'd find someone new fairly quickly but it didn't happen. My loneliness then had become a broader issue. It wasn't just about not fitting in, but also about not having found the right partner. I felt like I was surrounded by happily married friends producing children and I didn't want to be divorced and feeling like a failure. I wondered if I was doomed to be alone and single forever.

Even at times in my life when I haven't actually been feeling lonely, I've been *worrying* about feeling lonely. I've been fearful of the next event that *might* happen that *might* trigger those feelings of loneliness again.

My life has transformed over recent years. I've gone from that only child with no-one to play with to someone with a lot of close friends whom I see regularly. The 14 year age gap between my sister and me appears to get smaller with ever year that passes and we are becoming increasingly close. That best friend from my school days is *still* one of my closest friends but we don't really fall out anymore. I don't worry about the fact that other people enjoy partying and I don't: I just enjoy what I enjoy: a quiet

5

drink, dinner or simply a coffee with one or two of my closest friends. I don't worry *quite* so much when a relationship breaks down because I have such a good network of friends who help me pick up the pieces. I know marriage doesn't bring a guaranteed end to loneliness but I'm still hopeful that I might, one day, meet the right man. Now I'm in my 40s, I know it's unlikely that I'll have children of my own but I enjoy seeing my married friends and their children and I can enjoy being a good auntie! And I know, deep down, that even if I am "single forever", that doesn't mean being doomed to spend my life feeling lonely. Most importantly, I have grown to like me. I have worked out who I am and what I like doing – and what I don't like doing – and I have stopped trying so hard to be like other people and I am getting on with being myself. I still don't always feel like I quite "fit in" but I'm happy being my unique self.

This transformation, this move from feeling lonely to feeling content, didn't happen because of one single thing, one event, or one realisation. It seems to have happened slowly, step by step. Gradually, I made friends. Gradually, I became happy with who I am.

I don't think there is one easy idea that will help anyone and everyone go from feeling lonely to feeling contented. I'm not a psychologist or a doctor or an expert in any way. My only expertise lies in having been there, at the bottom of that rut of loneliness, and in having managed to crawl my way out of the rut. Perhaps not quite to the top just yet, but a good way up at any rate.

I've laid this book out in 52 short chapters. This layout was inspired by the book, *Everything I've Ever Done That Worked* by Lesley Garner. It's full of things that Lesley has tried, everything from using Bach Flower remedies to learning another language. The ideas in my book are things which I've tried and they're all things that have worked for me. They're gleaned from a variety of sources: books, the internet, conversations with other people and even a television programme or two. I quote these sources wherever possible, as a source of potential further reading and exploration. Personally, I've done a great deal of reading and much of it has helped me gain perspective on my loneliness – though admittedly, some of it hasn't helped at all.

I've done a great deal of talking too, to different people about my loneliness and theirs. I've been on a loneliness retreat and then started running loneliness retreats myself. I've discovered some things that work, some things that have really helped me to find freedom from loneliness. What surprises me most about these things is that they are all interconnected: for example, I discover that as I spend more time in silence and solitude, I learn to be more authentic and that in turn leads to both a rise in my self-esteem as well as more meaningful relationships and deeper connections with other people. It's a bit like the map of the London Underground: the Piccadilly Line crosses the Central Line and a little bit further along, it crosses the Northern Line, but the Northern Line intersects with the Central Line too.

The London Underground map feels like an appropriate analogy because, for me at least, finding freedom from loneliness has felt like a journey. Sometimes, on that journey, I've taken steps in the wrong direction or I've ended up going backwards. Sometimes, I feel like I've reached a dead end and I can't seem to move forwards. Sometimes I've felt that I've ended up right back where I started and, like all journeys, it hasn't always been easy.

I've written my ideas down for other people to read partly in the hope that it might help other people, partly because I find *meaning* in writing them down (see Idea 20) and finally to raise money for a good cause: my Help100 project, registered with the Inland Revenue as a small charity. In my Help100 project, I'm trying to help 100 people in a life-changing way. I'd like to think that perhaps one or more of the ideas in this book might prove to be life-changing for someone somewhere.

Seek professional help

A good therapist can help a lonely person in many ways…Essentially, the first benefit of psychotherapy is that it offers a confiding relationship to an individual who may lack other confidants.
~ Jacqueline Olds and Richard Schwartz

This book is not a substitute for professional help. I was too embarrassed to seek help, even from my friends, when I felt at my most lonely. I didn't then know anything of the damage that loneliness can do to a person's mental and physical health. "Loneliness, if prolonged, nearly always leads to depression," warn psychiatrists Jacqueline Olds and Richard Schwartz. But I didn't know that. I just thought I needed a few more friends.

But I did feel as if something was wrong with me and that was *why* I didn't have enough social contact. And that was why I didn't want to tell anyone.

Looking back, I realise that it would have been quite easy to seek professional help for my loneliness immediately after my divorce. I could have gone for counselling using the marital breakdown as an excuse and then broached the subject of loneliness.

The only help I did seek was going on a loneliness retreat at a religious institution. Having the chance to talk to a group of people who were also suffering from loneliness was invaluable. It was a safe environment and there was no fear of judgment. But it wasn't a substitute for therapy. I needed to talk to someone with an in-depth knowledge of loneliness and how to deal with it.

In *The Lonely Society,* the Mental Health Foundation's 2010 report into loneliness, it's suggested that "Clinical psychologists and psychiatrists can help people who feel lonely by addressing emotional issues that make it hard for them to form relationships or that reinforce their sense of isolation….If loneliness is linked to a deep anxiety about social situations, cognitive therapy could help to overcome that fear."

Although Cognitive Behavioural Therapy is available on the NHS, I just wasn't brave enough to approach my GP for help so I tried the DIY approach. My efforts revolved around increasing my self-esteem using the CBT techniques outlined in the books of Dr. David Burns, in particular *Ten Days to Great Self-Esteem* (see Idea 22).

This definitely had some effect, but I am sure that getting face-to-face help would have been more effective. I'm not alone in failing to seek help. In *The Lonely American*, Professor Jacqueline Olds states that many patients seeking help for anxiety or depression don't want to admit that their real problem is loneliness. "We found it was very difficult for our patients to talk about their isolation, which seemed to fill them with deep shame. We noticed they were far more comfortable saying they were depressed than lonely. The lonely word was determinedly avoided." According to *The Lonely Society*, "Some people might not seek the right psychological help because of their fear of being seen as a social failure."

I've got several close friends and lots of people who I'd put in the "friend/acquaintance" category. I am most definitely *not* a social failure. I'm just someone who feels lonely sometimes and there's nothing shameful in seeking help for that.

So I'll repeat: I'm not a psychiatrist, psychologist or expert in any way. This book is not a substitute for seeking professional help. It's simply a collection of ideas, a collection of the things that have helped me.

PART 1:
TAKE THE FIRST STEPS

Idea 1: Realise that you are not alone

Unhappiness …. comes to each of us because we think ourselves at the centre of the world, because we have the miserable conviction that we alone suffer to the point of unbearable intensity. Unhappiness is always to feel oneself imprisoned in one's own skin, in one's own brain.
~ Jacques Lusseyran,
Prisoner of Buchenwald Camp, World War II

I'm not comparing my experiences of feeling lonely because I'm single and don't always feel a sense of fitting in with the suffering endured in a World War 2 concentration camp.

But I did, until a few years ago, have the "miserable conviction" that I was the only person in the world who was suffering from feelings of loneliness and that conviction made my suffering worse.

It sounds like a cliché to say that you're not alone if you're feeling lonely but just realising that simple fact – that *other* people feel lonely too – was the biggest factor for me in overcoming my loneliness. Realising that loneliness is a common problem was my "Aha!" moment. It happened when suddenly, on impulse, I confessed to a friend in an email how lonely I felt and then she emailed back and said, "I feel that too!"

That one email opened my eyes to the fact that I'm not the only one. My friend is happily married, has lots of friends and has been successful in her job. She is valued by her bosses and her colleagues and is extremely fulfilled by the work she does. I thought that she was the last person on the planet who would feel lonely.

I had assumed loneliness was *my* problem. That it was just something I felt and it hadn't really occurred to me that anyone else felt it too. Not "normal" people anyway. Not people I liked, or worked with, or socialised with. Not people who seemed to be functioning normally in society, who were happily married, who had social lives and 200 friends on Facebook.

Loneliness has always made me feel that the way I feel inside is different from the way everyone else feels inside. Am I the only one who hasn't been invited to a party over the weekend? Who hasn't got friends coming to dinner or someone to see the latest film with at the cinema? Am I the only one who feels like she's spent a lifetime looking for Mr Right and never succeeding in finding him? Am I the only woman in her forties for whom God doesn't have a soulmate? And why doesn't he? Am I the only one who feels like she doesn't fit?

But this is far from being the case. I am far from being the only one. I found statistics that backed up this realisation that proved to me that this was not just *my* problem. According to the Mental Health Foundation's report, *The Lonely Society*, "Loneliness affects many of us at one time or another: only 22% of us never feel lonely and one in ten of us (11%) say we feel lonely often... A quarter of us (24%) worry about feeling lonely...Four in ten of us (42%) have felt depressed because we felt alone." If 22% of people *never* feel lonely, I realised that must mean that 78% of us will feel lonely at some point in our lives.

Society as a whole, I learned, is getting lonelier, and social psychologists have a whole realm of ideas as to why that is. I realised that I am *not* the problem. It is not that *I* don't fit in. It is not that *I* don't belong. It is not that *I* am strange or weird or not likeable or can't make friends or am not attractive enough to find a man or any of those other things that I had been secretly telling myself, secretly believing all those years. I have, like many people, an in-built capacity to feel lonely and I am living in an age and in a society where people are often lonely, perhaps lonelier than they have ever been before.

I know it's a cliché, but I really did feel as if the scales suddenly fell from my eyes. There was so much evidence that this was a common problem, not just *my* problem.

In the last few decades, there have been countless songs about loneliness. If loneliness was just my problem, then why would all those songs have been written? Roy

Orbison would hardly have sung about "Only the Lonely" or Hank Williams about "I'm so lonesome I could cry" if loneliness was just a problem that uniquely affected me. How could they? Roy and Hank hadn't even heard of Jennifer Page.

There are countless other examples I could have chosen: Andrew Gold's *Lonely Boy*, the Beatles' *Eleanor Rigby* or Elvis' *Are you lonesome tonight?* My personal favourite is Akon's *Mister Lonely*, which topped the charts in 2005 and samples Bobby Vinton's 1962 song of the same name. The original song, released during the Vietnam War, describes a soldier who is sent overseas and is missing home. For so many people to buy that record in 1962 and 2005, it must have had more than just a catchy tune: it must have struck a chord.

Amazon abounds with titles such as *Live Alone and Like It, Overcoming Loneliness and Making Friends, Single and Loving It* and *Positive Solitude*. I had read some of these and put others on my "wish list", but I hadn't somehow made the connection. I hadn't really internalised that knowledge, that belief, that if all those self-help books had been published and all those songs had been recorded about loneliness, then loneliness was a problem that was felt by millions of people. It wasn't unique to me at all.

It isn't surprising though that I missed all these signs. For every sign pointing to the fact that many people suffer from loneliness, there was a sign pointing the opposite way. For every song that has been written about feeling lonely, there's a sitcom or a drama series on TV featuring a group of happy friends or a happy family who do everything together and are always sitting around each others' kitchen tables, drinking endless coffees and sorting out each others' problems. I love watching *Frasier, Friends, Cold Feet* and *Mistresses* but they all feature these tight-knit groups and all have made me question, "Why don't I have friends like that? Why aren't I part of a group like that?"

I had focused on the wrong thing. Because of my loneliness, I had focused on the people who were seemingly enjoying what I was not enjoying. I hadn't noticed that in many of the novels I had enjoyed, there were many lonely characters that I could identify with. Mark Haddon's fantastic story, *The curious incident of the dog in the night time*, features a boy with Asperger's who seems to spend much of his time alone. *The Silver Linings Playbook* by Matthew Quick features a man struggling to cope with mental health problems following the breakdown of his marriage. In Claire Morrall's book, *The Language of Others*, the leading character Jessica has always felt a bit out of step with the world. Divorced, she is left living alone when her grown up son goes off to get married. I'd identified with – and liked – all of these characters – without ever thinking that the thing they had in common – and that I had in common with them - was their loneliness. Their feeling of being a little different, of not quite fitting in.

Suddenly, I began to notice signs of loneliness everywhere. Two well-known Christian retreat centres were offering "loneliness retreats". Films had central characters that were lonely – the wonderful *Lost in Translation*, for example, starring Billy Murray and Scarlett Johannson as two lonely people adrift in Tokyo. I had seen this film but somehow hadn't related their loneliness to mine until now. *You and Yours* on Radio 4 had a whole programme devoted to loneliness. The broadcaster Esther Rantzen wrote an article in the Daily Mail and went on *Woman's Hour,* explaining how she felt lonely. *She* felt lonely too?

I ventured into bookshops and libraries and looked for books on loneliness. Sometimes, I was too embarrassed to buy or borrow the books I found so I ordered them online when I got home, grateful for the anonymity of Amazon. Reading about loneliness was great. As I read, I discovered more people who felt like me and, what's more, who were willing to share their feelings.

I didn't feel strange anymore. My outlook changed over a few months. I no longer saw myself as someone who didn't fit in, who felt socially awkward at parties and who didn't feel quite "normal". I felt a new sense of belonging. I felt like I was part of a special new club, a club whose members were courageous enough and honest enough and authentic enough to own up to having these feelings of loneliness.

Admitting your loneliness is a huge step and a difficult one. On Radio 4's *Woman's Hour*, presenter Jane Garvey described loneliness as one of the last taboos in broadcasting. People are happy to go on TV chat shows and admit that they don't know who the father of their child is or that they've had sex with the grandfather of their best friend. Celebrities reveal details of their depression or their divorce in the tabloids. We watch all sorts of medical operations in intimate detail, we see every type of violence on our screens and we've even witnessed someone dying on TV. Yet we feel uncomfortable with those simple words, "I feel lonely."

The American writer Thomas Wolfe said, "The whole conviction of my life now rests upon the belief that loneliness, far from being a rare and curious phenomenon, peculiar to myself and to a few other solitary men, is the central and inevitable fact of human existence." I wish I had read that earlier and believed it, to understand that loneliness was just something that we human beings are prone to feeling. I wish I hadn't spent over 40 years of my life believing that there was something wrong with me.

Finally I stopped seeing myself as the cause of my loneliness, but that didn't mean that I saw myself as a victim of the lonely society in which I found myself. I wasn't the problem, I realised, but I could be the solution. I could *solve* this problem, or at least accept it, come to terms with it and stop allowing it to be such a big cause of suffering in my life.

Idea 2: Understand what loneliness is

Loneliness is an inner, gnawing pain born of circumstance and inertia, verging on despair. There is a higher risk the older you get, and no one talks about it.
~ Joan Bakewell, broadcaster

Once I'd had my "Aha!" moment and really started to believe that loneliness was not my problem but a natural consequence of me being human and living in the society in which I live, I began to think about what loneliness really is. I wanted to understand it more in the hope that understanding it might help me get to grips with it.

Of course, loneliness might mean different things to different people. It might mean not knowing what to do at Christmas if you are single and have no children to fill stockings for and no family to cook a Christmas lunch for. It might mean no wild parties to go to, because you're not really a party person and your friends aren't either. It might mean wondering who to spend your birthday with or go on holiday with or who might be free on Saturday night to go for a drink with. It might mean wondering who to share your problems with or who could go to the chemist to buy you some Lemsip when you've got the flu and can't get there yourself. It might mean wondering why you're the only person who is wandering down the high street on your own on a Saturday morning when everyone else is out in families or couples or groups of friends. It might mean being the only single person in your church whilst every other woman seems to have a child to drop off at Sunday school. It might simply mean having no-one to have a cup of tea and a natter with.

But loneliness isn't only about a lack of company. I wasn't always alone when I felt lonely. When I was married, there came a point when I simply felt I couldn't connect with my husband anymore. I am not laying the blame at anyone's door, it's just that the sense of connection had

17

simply gone. It seemed as if one night, I was lying in bed with him, watching him sleeping and thinking how lucky I was and the next, I was wondering where the love had gone to and why I didn't feel I could really talk to him anymore. I wasn't physically alone but I felt lonely. I've had that feeling at other times too. I've been out with a group of friends and suddenly felt like the odd one out for some reason I couldn't quite put my finger on. I've been at church, knowing I believed in God, but also knowing I didn't quite believe in God in the exactly the same way as everyone else did, but I was too afraid to share my feelings, in case they sounded like doubts. I've found myself at parties on many a Saturday night, surrounded by people drinking and dancing and listening to loud music and having a good time, and wondered why my idea of a good time did not include drinking, dancing and listening to loud music.

So what is loneliness exactly? What do I mean when I say that I am lonely?

The definitions I have found don't feel that helpful. The Oxford English Dictionary online describes loneliness as "sadness because one has no friends or company" or "the fact of being without companions". In *Positive Solitude*, Rae Andre describes loneliness as "…not an emotion but a word people use to summarise their experience of the problem emotions they feel when they are alone." In both cases, I don't find this helpful because it overlooks the fact that we can feel lonely when we are not objectively alone. It's that old cliché of "lonely in a crowd". I can be in a room full of people, people that I know, and still feel desperately lonely. I can spend an entire weekend alone in the house and see no-one and feel totally happy.

Whilst loneliness obviously *might* be experienced by someone who is physically alone, it is a subjective experience. Many people, like me, are capable of feeling completely content when alone but extremely lonely in a room full of other people. Being with someone with whom I don't feel a strong sense of connection can make me feel very isolated indeed: for example, staying in a relationship when things are going wrong. As I read on one blog,

"When have I felt most lonely? Oh I know the answer to that one: lying in bed next to the girl that I loved but who I felt didn't love me."

That's the paradox of loneliness. It cannot be easily explained. It is still most often associated with the state of being physically, objectively alone, yet many people still feel lonely when they are with people. John Cacioppo is the director of the Center for Cognitive and Social Neuroscience at the University of Chicago and the author of *Loneliness: Human Nature and the Need for Social Connection.* He defines loneliness as "the feeling that you're socially isolated. It's related to being physically isolated from other people, but it's not the same thing. One can be lonely in a marriage, lonely in a family…"

If curing loneliness was purely and simply a question of spending enough time in the company of other people, I'd be able to sort myself out pretty easily. Join the local running club, go salsa dancing more often, make arrangements to see my friends and get involved in one of the many groups on Meetup. But it's much more complicated than that. I feel lonely if I'm in the wrong relationship, but still find it difficult to leave that relationship as being alone might make me feel even lonelier. It seems that even the right relationship is no guarantee of a contented life free of loneliness: one of my friends is happily married and yet still experiences times of great loneliness. Loneliness is just so difficult to define, so difficult to put your finger on and therefore so difficult to do something about.

When lonely people talk about their feelings, they often talk of feeling distanced or disconnected from those around them and the best way I can describe what I perceive of as loneliness is "the feelings of sadness or hopelessness that I feel when I lack a sense of connection."

I might experience that lack of connection when I'm home alone and have no-one to connect with, but it might just as easily be felt when I'm sitting opposite a friend and, for some inexplicable reason, the usually warm feelings of friendship and companionship are missing. Perhaps the conversation isn't flowing like it usually does. Perhaps I'm simply not in the right frame of mind. It might be when I'm at a party and there's no-one I know to talk to or it might be when I'm sitting in the office thinking that actually, this job is pretty futile and not what I want to be doing with the rest of my life. It might be when I see a father playing with his children in the park and I wish that I'd had my own children or it might be when I see a beautiful sunset and wish I had someone to turn to and say simply, "Wow, that's a beautiful sunset."

Arriving at a definition of *my* loneliness as a "lack of connection" allowed me to see a solution. I had to find ways of making that connection. I had felt hopeless. I didn't know where to turn or what to do to help myself. Because I didn't know how to express the thing that was *missing*, I didn't know what I was looking for. Once I identified "connection" as the missing ingredient in my life, I felt better. I knew that "connection" would give me the sense of belonging, of feeling right, of being comfortable in my own skin.

Idea 3: Make connections

We long to love and be loved but find ourselves frustrated by
steel doors of loneliness.
~ Gerard Hughes

Defining loneliness as a "lack of connection" allowed me to see that the solution to my loneliness is to establish connections.

The obvious type of connection that might ease my loneliness, I decided, was to form more connections and *deeper* connections with other people. That might mean making new friendships, but it might also mean putting time into existing friendships so that those friendships could grow from being superficial into something more meaningful and satisfying.

But when I'm feeling lonely, forming connections with other people seems, quite frankly, about as possible as someone who gets out of breath walking round the local park suddenly jumping up and climbing Everest. If I'm in on my own on a Friday night, without a single invitation in my social diary, forming connections with other people seems like something that is just beyond my capability. I feel like I've failed before I have even started.

It's a classic catch 22 situation. The lonelier I get, the more I need to make those connections with other people, but the more daunting it seems to actually go and find people. When I do manage to go out, I feel needy and clingy. I "try too hard" at parties, hoping to make a good impression and walk away with a collection of new friends. The trouble is that when I try that hard, other people sense it and back away. I go out with high expectations – perhaps at this lecture or dinner or meeting or whatever, I'll meet Mr Right and that will be the end of all my problems. When I arrive, I scan the room, see mostly single women just like me, and I realise that it's not going to happen. Then I'm in too much of a grumpy mood to bother making connections with those women.

If I can manage to get myself off the sofa and out of the front door, I've realised, the key is to leave my high expectations behind. I try to go with an open mind – this time I might meet a new friend, but I might not. I might meet the man of my dreams, but I might not. I might spend a fantastic evening having lots of interesting conversations at the party, but actually I might also be a wallflower and spend a lot of time feeling nervous and insecure. By not having high expectations, I'm less likely to come home deflated and disappointed, vowing never to go to another party or singles night or meeting ever again. I'll come home accepting that the connection I was looking for hasn't happened this time but it *could* happen next time.

But, I realised, it wasn't just connection with other people that might ease my loneliness. At times when other people aren't available for company, being in tune with my inner self, being *connected* to my inner self, means that I'm able to tap into some inner resource of strength. I've heard people describe this as self-love. If you can't love yourself, I've been told, you can't really love someone else.

That relationship with yourself, with who you really are, is crucial. If I don't like someone, I won't enjoy spending an evening with them. If I don't like who I am, then I probably won't enjoy an evening with myself either. Basically, I won't enjoy spending time on my own. If I am really connected to myself, if I really know and understand myself, I'll understand what makes me feel contented and fulfilled. So I'll focus on doing *those* things when I'm by myself, rather that turning to things that leave me feeling empty, bored and even more isolated, like drinking too much wine or watching non-stop television for hours on end.

Connection with the world around me is also important. Within the four walls of my house, I can feel lonely, isolated. Going out into the garden and digging for an hour makes me feel connected again. Often, a robin joins me, greedily picking up the worms that my fork has unearthed. That robin's appearance makes me feel less lonely. Going for a walk, going to feed the ducks or simply appreciating the colour or scent of a flower somehow eases my loneliness. Somehow I feel part of something bigger. It isn't just me, alone in the world. I am *part* of that world, connected to it.

Finally, connection with God, with some higher power, also eases my loneliness. Of course, not everyone has that sense of God, not everyone believes in God. But for me, my belief in God is a real source of comfort. I feel safe in the knowledge that even when I am physically alone, I am not spiritually alone.

So I began to explore practical things I could do to increase my sense of connectedness in all of these four aspects: a connection with my inner self, more frequent and more meaningful connections with other people, a closer connection with the natural world and a deeper connection with God. My quest to find freedom from loneliness had become a search for connections.

PART 2:
FIND A CONNECTION TO
YOUR INNER SELF

Idea 4: Accept that you might need other people

People who need people are the luckiest people in the world.
~ From the musical *Funny Girl*

It might seem strange to start a section on finding a connection to yourself with a chapter on accepting that you need other people, but if I perceive my loneliness as a sadness that can be caused by a lack of connection to other people, then I have to acknowledge that part of myself which needs to have meaningful connections – relationships – with other human beings.

In the story of my journey out of loneliness, this was where I fell at the first hurdle. Everyone was telling me that I should be revelling in the fact that I'm an independent woman who doesn't need anyone else. So many of the self-help books I read seemed to be telling me that it was ok to be alone, that really, I ought to like it. Amazon lists no less than three books by three different authors with the words "single and loving it" in the title. There are even more books on living alone and loving it. Apparently, I should be feeling empowered, I should be getting on and enjoying life. I'm slightly embarrassed to admit that my bookshelves are overflowing with such titles: over the years, I've devoured them, believing them to hold the answers to my emptiness, but one by one, the books disappointed me. I tried to believe the theory, but I couldn't.

Let's be honest about it. You're single and you'd rather not be, you've lost someone close, you've moved to a new area or you've simply never felt like you've fitted in – for whatever reason, you feel lonely and isolated and that is a pretty difficult state to learn to enjoy. It simply doesn't feel right for much of the time. I might as well face up to the fact that I wish someone would send me a Valentine's card on Valentine's Day or surprise me with flowers on my birthday. I wish someone would call me mummy. I wish I was the apple of someone's eye and that my mere presence made someone's heart flutter.

Deep down, I felt lonely because I longed for a sense of connection, a really deep connection, with other people. Yet I felt as though these books were telling me that I was wrong to be seeking that. If I was a normal, fully-functioning human being, they would have me believe, I *should* be able to be perfectly happy on my own. I believed these books. I believed that there was some flaw in me, some shortfall somewhere, that stopped me from enjoying being alone and independent and that meant that whilst I needed other people, the rest of the world did not.

Society puts such a high value on independence. Being independent is a personal quality worth striving for. People on internet dating sites write the word "independent" proudly, hoping that it makes them more attractive to members of the opposite sex. I think I even wrote it on my profile. But I didn't feel independent. I found myself buying books on "co-dependency" and wondering if the problem was that I was co-dependent. I even went to a CODA meeting, the twelve step programme for people with relationship issues. I listened to an alcoholic friend describing his addictive need for alcohol and identified my own need for relationships as having similarly unhealthy patterns. I remembered helpful friends suggesting that I learned to live on my own and enjoy it before I got into another romantic relationship. I remembered my old school reports where teachers would suggest that I made more of an effort to be "independent" and recalled how my Spanish tutor at university had slipped me a copy of the book *Women Who Love Too Much*, after I'd blubbed my way through a tutorial after yet another relationship break-up.

I felt caught between two opposite poles. My heart was telling me that I wanted – that I needed – meaningful relationships with other people in order to feel happy and fulfilled. Yet these books were telling me that I *shouldn't* need these relationships. In fact, some of them went a step further. They suggested that I could not have happy and fulfilled relationships with other people *until* I was completely happy and independent and didn't need anyone else. I felt like a tennis ball being batted between the opposite ends of the court.

For the last ten years, author Sara Maitland has been living on her own, almost entirely in solitude and silence. Despite her social isolation, her life is far from being miserable. As she told the Guardian newspaper that "my life, in its contours at the moment, is more exciting and more interesting than that of most of my peers."

I loved Sara's account of her solitary life, *A Book of Silence*, and found it totally inspiring, but that didn't mean that Sara's ability to be completely content on her own was something that *I* should aspire to. It's this idea that I think blocked my release from loneliness for so long: the idea that I am somehow abnormal for wanting social interaction and deep friendships with other people, for wanting company. Most people probably *couldn't* live the life that Sara leads and be content. According to scientists, the majority of us *do* have some level of need for connection with other human beings. We're social animals. When psychologist John Cacioppo was asked about whether people really need social interactions, he said that if a zookeeper was designing an enclosure suitable for humans, he would need to be warned of the 'obligatory social gregariousness of our species.' Keeping humans in an environment where they were unable to socialise with each other would be as unthinkable as putting hippos in a pen without water or monkeys in a cage with nothing to swing from. We are hard-wired to want to be with other people because, on the wild plains of Africa many millennia ago, we were simply safer in a group than on our own. As Genesis 2:18 says, "It is not good for man to be alone."

Sometimes I'm told by well-meaning friends that I should just enjoy being single. "The right person will come along when you're least expecting it," they tell me cheerfully. Perhaps they are right. But not everyone's experiences of being alone are the same. Just as some people need more food than others, some people need more company. According to social psychologists and neuroscientists, we don't all have identical needs when it comes to how much time we like spending on our own. We are hard-wired with *different* levels of need for connection with other people. We don't all have the same upbringing and the way we're brought up leaves us with different expectations of how much social connection we *should* have in life. That explains why one of my friends *has* to have somewhere to go and someone to be with every single night of the week whilst Sara Maitland's idea of heaven seems to be living alone in the middle of nowhere without even a television for company.

However, the scientists agree that *most* people need to spend some time in the company of others and that need is as basic as our need to eat and sleep. I am normal, I realise. Well, in that aspect at least!

Realising that it's normal to want to spend time with others felt like big news to me. I felt that I had *permission* to need other people in my life. It was no longer wrong to acknowledge that I would like friendships and relationships and that I wanted to connect with other human beings. It was no longer an admission of failure to not be 100% independent and it was a huge relief not to have to go round pretending that I was. I don't have to spend long periods of time all on my own and act like that is perfectly ok and that I'm enjoying it, when I'm not. I can stop judging myself for needing other people. There is nothing at all wrong or abnormal with wanting other people in my life. They can be a great source of joy, love and companionship.

Suddenly, I realised that overcoming my loneliness was not about becoming a person who didn't *need* other people. One key to overcoming my loneliness was simply *accepting* my need to spend time in other people's company and finding a way to have more of it.

Idea 5: Find your authentic self

Why do we have to spend our lives striving to be something we would never want to be, if we only knew what we wanted? Why do we waste our time doing things which, if we only stopped to think about them, are just the opposite of what we were made for?
~ Thomas Merton

I was 19 when I first realised that I was putting on an act and that it was putting on that act that led me to feel disconnected from others. It was ironic as sometimes I was putting on the act in order to try to make myself more acceptable to others, in the hope of making a connection, in the hope of making friends.

In my first year at university, it was the Christmas do of the students' Methodist Society. I fancied John, who was in his third year of a law degree. But I was still a virgin, I'd barely been kissed and I didn't have a clue about men.

What's more, I felt socially awkward. What if no-one spoke to me and John saw that? He might deduce that I was unlikeable. I might be seen as a bit of a loser, and he'd never fancy me then. I really didn't know how to get into conversations with people. I couldn't do that small talk you're supposed to do at parties. I felt ill at ease. I was dressed wrong. I had dressed up in an effort to look nice but all the other girls were managing to look nice in jeans and t-shirts. I knew people there but I didn't know anyone enough just to walk up to them and begin a conversation. In desperation, so as not to appear at a loose end, I asked the minister's wife if I could help get the drinks or something.

As soon as I had a job to do, I felt okay. I felt that all-important sense of belonging and I tried to appear confident and efficient, asking everyone if they wanted tea or coffee. I felt successful – I even dared to make a few jokes and the whole room laughed. I was even beginning to think that I looked ok too – just slightly overdressed. I

30

couldn't understand why John didn't ask me for a date at the end of the evening.

A few weeks later, after Christmas, it was the university ballroom dancing trials. I had a partner, Mike, whom I often danced with and I longed for us to make the team. I bought a new outfit – a swirling purple skirt and matching top – and did my hair and make-up. For once, I thought that I looked pretty good. It was unusual for me to feel that confident about my appearance. I looked in the mirror and actually liked what I saw.

The trials' format was simple. It took the form of a social dance with the judges looking on to see who caught their eye. They'd put on a waltz and everyone found a partner and waltzed. A cha cha and people partnered up and did a cha cha.

The trouble was that no-one asked me to dance. Not one person. Mike was dancing with Angela, a girl far more attractive than me who was in her first year studying French. She was so attractive that she hadn't needed to get dressed up: a bit like the girls at the Christmas party, she was just in t-shirt and jeans.

Naturally I wasn't picked for the trials. Of course I wasn't. The judges hadn't even seen me dance. Angela was. She and Mike were picked to dance together.

A week later was Valentine's Day. I got no cards. Not one. I was walking to lectures and who should I see but Angela. The last person I wanted to see. I bet she's been inundated with cards and flowers, I thought jealously. I made up my mind to rush past her but she said hello and stopped, clearly wanting to talk. Wanting to brag, I thought, about all those cards she's got. And sure enough, her first question was, "How many Valentine's cards did you get?"

I couldn't think fast enough to lie and found myself mumbling, "None."

To my surprise, Angela said, "Me neither. I thought *you'd* get loads!"

"No," I said. "I thought *you'd* get loads of cards!"

Suddenly we were consoling each other and I had made a connection. Angela became one of the few people I could really call a friend at university. She had dared to be vulnerable, to be honest, to admit the truth to me, and I was able to be truthful back.

I congratulated her on making the ballroom dancing team and she said how sorry she was that I hadn't made it too.

"Well, no-one even asked me to dance," I said wistfully. "I thought I looked good."

"You looked too good," said Angela. "You looked perfect. All the men were too scared to approach you!"

Of course, I'll never know if she was right or if she was just being generous and trying to make me feel better. But I realised soon afterwards that both my act of confidence at the Methodists' party and my efforts to dress up rather than just wearing clothes that I was comfortable in were attempts to act like someone I wasn't. They were totally counterproductive too. By acting this way, I didn't attract John or Mike. In fact, I put them off. They might have liked the real me a bit more than the overdressed me, who was full of fake confidence.

The late Steve Jobs, founder of Apple, put this better than I possibly could. In his famous commencement speech at Stanford University in 2005, he said: "Remembering that I'll be dead soon is the most important tool I've ever encountered to help me make the big choices in life. Because almost everything — all external expectations, all pride, all fear of embarrassment or failure – these things just fall away in the face of death, leaving only what is truly important. Remembering that you are going to die is the best way I know to avoid the trap of thinking you have something to lose. You are already naked. There is no reason not to follow your heart."

I am already naked, I realised. I am already vulnerable. It was only when I dared to *be* vulnerable and naked and admit to another human being that I had no Valentine's cards and was feeling rejected, that I actually made a true friend at university. For me, being naked means not putting on an act or trying to impress other people, but just having the courage to be myself.

32

"Who are you?" asks Jenny Bristow, author of *Single and Loving It*, "Without a partner. Without the role of girlfriend, wife, 'other half'. Now you're half of nothing, you're one whole of a whole. But what shape is that whole? What colour is it? What does it like to do? What tune does it like to dance to?"

I realize that I have spent my life being what *other* people expected me to be. A well-behaved child. A good student at school. A party-animal at university (well, I didn't quite manage that one but I tried!) A hard-working teacher, when really I longed to be an opera singer or work in TV. A devoted TV researcher, when really I was itching to make it as a producer. A good wife. The less said about that one the better. A great girlfriend. Ditto. I'm not sure when I ever tried just to be me. Or when I simply stopped trying altogether.

"Many people in our society are actually extremely lonely," say psychiatrists Jacqueline Olds and Richard Schwartz, "not because they lack contact with people but because they have no-one with whom they can truly 'be themselves', no-one with whom they can talk about almost anything with little self-consciousness..... When a person has friends and acquaintances, but no-one with whom he is 'truly himself', the loneliness that results can wither creativity, exploration and even the necessary actions required to keep life moving along."

That view is echoed by Robert Waldron in *15 days of prayer with Henri Nouwen*: "To become intimate with people, we risk being hurt; consequently, we often wear personae (masks) to camouflage our real selves, but when we become comfortable (and safe) wearing them, we fail to connect with others on an intimate level; our relationships are, therefore, superficial."

Learning to be myself, dropping the mask behind which I normally hide, sounds easier than it actually is. People often say, "Just be yourself Jenny!" if I ask for advice when I'm about to go for a job interview or I'm going off on a date. But I don't think I'm alone in not being completely sure of who that "real me", that "authentic self" really is.

Paul McKenna, in his book *Change Your Life in Seven Days,* says that our truest, most authentic selves are like diamonds. We cover these diamonds up somehow with layers of negative self-image: "the shame, fear and guilt, the person we're afraid we are." These layers cover the beauty of our innermost selves, of the diamond, like layers of horse manure. Then, because we sense that those layers aren't so attractive, we cover them up with yet more layers, trying to pretend that we are someone other than who we really are, because we're afraid that we're not good enough. It is, he says, the equivalent of attempting to cover the horse manure with a layer of nail varnish. Instead, we should chip away at the manure until we see the diamond underneath.

We are wrapped "with the bandages of the false self, like the Invisible Man being wrapped mummy-like in long-winding strips of cloth" as James Martin puts it in *Becoming Who We Are..* That's James Martin the Jesuit priest, *not* the celebrity chef. But *how* do we chip the manure off that diamond? *How* do we remove those bandages?

In *Travelling Light,* Daniel O'Leary makes the following suggestion:

> …reflect on your feelings and reactions at times of criticism, disapproval or rejection. These are the moments when the ego and its tricks are evident. Notice the denial, the defence, the self-pity that immediately rush in. This, in fact, goes on all the time and makes our lives inauthentic and miserable. Notice too our reaction to praise, to winning, to being proved right. We are over the moon, so very happy. The ego is having a field-day in both instances. These examples mean that we are finding our identity only in our achievements, our possessions and the approval of others. It is to see our worth only through the eyes of others; to be over-dependent. There is no inner centre, no grounded self. The journey ahead is about

becoming less self-centred, less touchy and prickly, less gullible and fearful. But for the moment, just pay attention to the self-importance of the ego on the stage of today's experiences, whether these be positive or negative. And don't forget to enjoy the show!

I knew as soon as I read those words that it was a fairly accurate description of me. I am far too dependent on the approval of others. I see my worth in terms of my achievements. For example, I used to feel a sense of pride because I owned a sports car. Sadly, unemployment forced me to get rid of it, but I liked the car because I thought it made me look like I'd made it. But, I realise, this is not the "real me" – it's just my ego. Could letting go of that ego and finding that authentic self help my feelings of loneliness?

In 1958, the psycho-analyst Donald Winnicott published a paper on 'The Capacity to Be Alone.' Commenting on this work, psychiatrist Anthony Storr noted that Winnicott was "particularly preoccupied with whether an individual's experience was authentic or inauthentic."

> Many of the patients whom he treated had, for one reason or another, learned as children to be over-compliant; that is, to live in ways which were expected of them, or which pleased others, or which were designed not to offend others. These are the patients who build up what Winnicott called a 'false self'; that is, a self which is based upon compliance with the wishes of others, rather than being based upon the individual's own true feelings and instinctive needs. Such an individual ultimately comes to feel that life is pointless and futile, because he is merely adapting to the world rather than experiencing it as a place in which his subjective needs can find fulfillment... He suggests that the capacity to be alone ... is related to the

individual's capacity to get in touch with, and make manifest, his own true inner feelings.

I realised early on in my quest to find freedom from loneliness that it would be a spiritual journey, a question of delving deep into myself and discovering who I am, why I believe what I believe, why I do what I do and how to shake off any beliefs, habits and patterns of thinking that are simply not helpful to me.

"If you're ever going to be free, you must be willing to prove to yourself that your inherent nature is goodness, that when you stop doing everything else, goodness is what's there," says Cheri Huber, a teacher of Zen awareness practice and author of *There Is Nothing Wrong With You*. "You'll never prove that to yourself as long as you're beating yourself...You must find the courage to stop beating yourself long enough to find out that who you are is goodness. This is why we have meditation practice: to learn to sit still with whatever is happening."

I learnt to be myself simply by just sitting still with myself. It sounds ridiculous. I didn't understand what the books were telling me at first. I didn't recognise when I was being my true self and when I was being my false self. I just concentrated on what I was really feeling. I just accepted that that was how I was feeling.

As I finally learn to be my authentic self on my own, I begin to be able to allow that authentic self to reveal herself to other people, and I am a little bit further along the road to finding freedom from loneliness.

Idea 7: Don't just sit there – do something

Action is consolatory. It is the enemy of thought and the friend of flattering illusions.
~ Joseph Conrad

Everyone today rushes round saying they have no time and I am no exception. I don't have enough time for all the things I want to do in life, either on a day to day basis, or on a longer term basis. For example, I'd like to run, pray or meditate, write my blog, keep the house tidy and cook meals from scratch every single day, but even on a good day, I probably only manage two of those. On a longer term basis, I'd like to keep up with my friends, do a good job at work, have a decent holiday somewhere adventurous once a year, go to interesting events, start a business and write my next book. But there's never time to fit it all in.

Yet the paradox is that there are times when I find myself at a loose end. I have a weekend when my housemate is away and all my friends are busy doing other things. There are no events to go to and nowhere I have to be. Those are the days when loneliness strikes.

You would think then that on those empty days, I would manage to write my blog, pray, go for a run, tidy the house *and* do something towards those longer term goals such as writing a chapter or drawing up a business plan.

Those days don't work like that. Those are the days when I get up and feel miserable because it's a Saturday and I have nowhere to go and everyone else does. Everyone else has somewhere to go and someone to be with. Except me. Self-pity and loneliness set in with a vengeance. Those are the days when I end up on the sofa watching back to back episodes of *Come Dine with Me* on More4. They are usually episodes I've already seen and I inevitably remember who cooked what, who fell out with whom and who won. In other words, watching them again has very little point.

Maybe watching them in the first place didn't have much point, but I'll save that discussion for Idea 8.

Finding the motivation, the inner resources, to deal with this empty time doesn't come easily to me.

Boredom and then loneliness take a firm hold of me and they get inside my head and take root. I've read about strange and terrifying parasites in foreign countries that invade the human body. They get in through various orifices - I'm sure I've read somewhere that one gets into your bladder through your urethra and I've been cautious about swimming in tropical waters ever since. They have hooks that embed themselves into your flesh. That is why they are difficult to rip out – they take part of your flesh with them.

Well, on empty days, particularly weekend days or worse still, bank holidays, when it feels like everyone else has something exciting to do apart from me, loneliness is like that parasite that sneaks into me and hooks itself inside me, making it very difficult to get out.

It's hard to get motivated. Although sitting on the sofa watching TV is not making me happy, I cannot seem to find the energy to do something that *might* make me happy. It's like when people tell you to "just get out more" – you know it might help, but doing it isn't as easy as people make out.

In her book *Everything I've Ever Done That Worked*, Lesley Garner's advice for dealing with the little jobs you've put off for ages like your tax return or clearing out the loft is to do one of those tasks for 20 minutes. Just 20 minutes. Set yourself that goal. Apparently, it then doesn't seem as arduous as asking yourself to do the whole tax return so you're much more likely to get started. The chances are that once you've done 20 minutes, you might feel like carrying on and finishing it. And if you don't, you just stop. You don't feel bad because you've done what you set out to do: 20 minutes of that tax return done. At least you've done some of it.

I've found that the 20 minute tactic works just as well when I'm in my bored, lonely, I-don't-want-to-do-anything-except-watch-*Come-Dine-With-Me* mood, as it does when I'm in my I-don't-want-to-do-my-tax-return mood. It really works. I go for a 20 minute run, I feel energised. I clear out the wardrobe for just 20 small minutes and I feel instantly uplifted by the difference that I've made.

There's something about taking action that lifts my mood and my loneliness leaves me, taking his best buddy boredom with him.

Idea 8: Turn off the TV

Being busy, active and on the move has nearly become part
of our constitution. When we are asked to sit in a chair,
without a paper to read, a radio to listen to, a television to watch,
without a visitor or a phone, we are inclined to become
so restless and tense that we welcome anything that will distract
us again. This explains why silence is such a difficult task.
~ Henri Nouwen, *Reaching Out*

TV is definitely part of my constitution. When I first got divorced, I had the TV on all the time. Whenever I got home, the first thing I'd do would be to switch it on. If I was moving around from room to room, I'd put it on quite loudly, so that I could hear it as I went about the house. If I was sitting on the sofa answering my emails, I'd put the TV on for "company". Even if I got home at midnight after a night out, on a day when I had work the next morning, I'd still watch a TV programme before going to bed. I'd record things so that there was always something to watch. TV was my security blanket.

One of the programmes I watched during that time was called *Making Slough Happy*. The premise of the programme was that Slough was the unhappiest place in the UK. The people in Slough were therefore deemed to be the unhappiest people in the UK and a group of psychologists set out, using positive psychology and the newly invented "science of happiness" to try and make the whole town happier. Since I was unhappy too, I figured that whatever those psychologists were doing to Slough to make Slough happier, I could probably implement in my own life to make *me* happier. Every week, I'd video the programme and every week I'd sit down eagerly to see what I ought to be doing.

There were about ten things to do, ten pieces of wisdom if you like, in the "Happiness Manifesto", but I was really unhappy about one of them: watch half as much TV.

40

The TV was my crutch at the time. I couldn't contemplate turning it off.

Yet try as I might, I couldn't ignore the "Happiness Manifesto", backed up as it was by a whole heap of evidence. There's evidence, for example, that links the amount of TV that people watch with their levels of obesity. There's evidence suggesting a link between TV watching habits and Attention Deficit Disorder in children and there's research that suggests that people who watch a lot of television report a lower degree of life satisfaction. An article in the Journal of Economic Psychology in 2007, based on the European Social Survey, reported that people who watched less than half an hour of TV a day were more satisfied with their life than those who watched more. Of course, it might not be that the TV viewing is causing the lack of satisfaction: perhaps unhappy people watch more TV than happy people.

Perhaps we're drawn to watching TV because it's easy. I don't have to get up off my sofa, or pluck up courage to venture into a new place on my own, or do anything too strenuous or tiring.

According to psychologist Mihály Csíkszentmihályi, "The mood state Americans are in, on average, when watching television is mildly depressed." He believes that more engaging activities such as working out at the gym or taking on a new project require you to cross over some kind of threshold. Watching TV, on the other hand, is just instant gratification and because of that, it's less satisfying.

Or as author Gretchen Rubin puts it, "It's the difference between settling in with a bag of potato chips versus taking the time to make a nutritious meal…. In terms of hours, watching TV is probably the world's most popular pastime. Among Americans, it's the most common free-time activity – for an average of about five hours a day. It's a source of relaxing fun. But while television is a good servant, it's a bad master. It can swallow up huge quantities of our lives, without much happiness bang for the buck."

But TV was such a comfort, in the years following my divorce. I hated being lonely, but being *bored* and lonely

41

was even worse, and the TV seemed to offer a way out of boredom. Only it didn't. At the end of an evening's viewing, I would feel dissatisfied. I wondered: is there more to life than this?

Soap operas really sapped my time and I became engrossed in the characters' lives. Whilst Gail, Audrey, Sally and Kevin all felt like old friends, they were no substitute for the real thing. Although I did once sit next to Kevin – or at least the actor who played him – when I was in reception at Granada TV, waiting for a job interview. The trouble is, as I've already pointed out, the characters in soap operas, dramas and sit-coms tend to live in happy families or groups of friends, who flit easily in and out of each others' lives and homes and that just made me feel abnormal. *Friends, Frasier* and *Sex and the City* all left me wondering why I wasn't part of a group like that, when it felt like the rest of the world was.

"If one believes that television is a 'window to the world,' then watching television is how that person connects with the world around them. The reality is that by watching television, you do not really connect with any other living people - you only really establish a relationship with your television set," says Ron Kaufman, in "The Zen of Television", on the website turnoffyourtv.com.

I don't think that my habit of watching too much TV is entirely to blame for my loneliness. As someone who has spent most of her working life making TV programmes, I'm kind of bound to say that. But I do think that our attachment to TV, our dependence on it, can cause us problems.

"Television watching," says Robert E Lane in his book *The Loss of Happiness in Market Democracies*, "may be a substitute for friendly discourse….Like a pet, the television set and its programmes represent a form of companionship." Television watching deduces Lane, "is a cause of isolation as well as an effect."

In other words, you are more likely to watch lots of TV if you feel lonely, but watching lots of TV can cause your loneliness. However, Lane does acknowledge that television "may bring family members together and could be an occasion for social interaction."

The idea of TV as something that might actually bring people together was something I first came across in a book written by Stuart Hall. That's Stuart Hall the media theorist not the presenter of *It's a Knockout*. Whilst some people argue that TV is to blame for the death of real conversation in our society, others point out that TV itself can be a starting point for conversation. How many Monday mornings begin in offices up and down the country with the words, "Who saw the *X Factor* on Saturday? Could you believe that?" How many friendships have started because of a shared love of *The Apprentice*? Or *Strictly Come Dancing*? Sometimes, being the only person who doesn't watch *The X Factor* has left me feeling completely excluded.

"TV," says Gretchen Rubin again, "lets you chat with people around the water cooler. It provides a way to gossip without being hurtful. It can be a source of expertise, a way to be knowledgeable…..Watching TV is companionable. When the Big Man and I watch *The Office*, we feel like we're doing something together. We've having the same experience, in a way that we aren't if we're both reading or working". The bottom line is, according to Gretchen, that "…if you watch TV *mindfully* and *purposefully*, it can be a source of happiness, especially if you use it to connect with other people. If you watch it passively, automatically, and for want of anything better to do, it can be a drain on happiness."

As a pre-school child, I loved Monday lunchtimes. My mother would make us egg and chips and we would watch the programme *Mr and Mrs* together as we ate. It was a ritual that I loved. It was something that my mother and I *shared*. During the evenings too, we'd watch TV together as a family, enjoying the same shows and laughing at the same things: *Dad's Army, Are You Being Served?* and *The Good Life*.

By the time my sister arrived, some 14 years after I'd been born, our household, like many others, had gone from being a one-television-set household to a three-television-set household. My sister often chose, as a child, to watch TV alone in one room, whilst we watched a different channel in another. I am not criticising my sister for this: in fact, I'm sorry that she didn't have the shared experience of family TV viewing that I enjoyed. I'm not criticising my parents either: it was what everyone was doing. More and more children were getting TV sets in their rooms and living isolated little lives watching their own programmes or playing on their games consoles, whilst the grown-ups watched something different elsewhere. Perhaps this change is inevitable. When I was little, there were only 3 TV channels to choose from. Now there are hundreds. It just seems sad that we humans opt for watching the programme that we really want to watch in a room on our own, rather than watching a programme that other people want to watch and enjoying their companionship. Since when did spending time with a box of electronics become more important than spending time with our loved ones?

Another childhood memory is watching the children's programme *Why Don't You…?* A group of young people would show viewers interesting things that they could do : things to make, hobbies to try and places to visit. The full title of the programme was *Why Don't You Just Switch Off Your TV Set And Go And Do Something Less Boring Instead?* There's a danger when I'm feeling lonely, demotivated and perhaps even depressed to just switch the TV on and wile away the hours. Yet that's the very time when I need to get out there and do something less boring instead.

So I recently experimented with a week of no TV. At first it was hard. I no longer live alone, but when I'm at home on my own, I like to turn the TV on whilst I have my dinner, to give myself the illusion of company. When I wasn't going out in an evening, I wasn't quite sure what to do with myself. But just like *Why Don't You* said, I soon discovered that turning off the TV set did indeed make me do something less boring instead. I soon discovered that it made a nice change to sit in a hot bubble bath surrounded by candles for an hour or so, that having an early night with a good book and a mug of hot chocolate was rather lovely and one evening, I even found myself creating a piece of art. Admittedly, it's not Michelangelo but I enjoyed the act of creating it.

And did those activities help my loneliness? Yes, I think they probably did. I was simply too busy to feel lonely. (Though I'd caution against being *too* busy – that's also been the cause of some of my loneliness! See Idea 21)

Idea 9: Keep a journal

*An incredibly powerful healing tool is already in your hands
which costs no more than the price of a biro and a piece of paper. It's
called writing. The sheer simplicity of putting feelings down on paper
has benefits out of proportion to the act itself.*
~ Jenny Bristow, *Single and Loving It*

A few weeks before my ex-husband and I separated, but when I had already guessed that our separation was on the cards, I came across a short article in a Sunday newspaper. The article described 10 things that you should do to help yourself through a divorce. I don't remember what nine of the things were, but the idea of keeping a journal stuck in my head.

I remembered that advice during the first lonely, sleepless night without my ex. I had kept a diary as a child, but as an adult with a busy life, the effort of keeping a daily journal had been too much and my efforts had been sporadic. But that night, I got out my work notebook and began filling the empty pages with my thoughts and feelings. I haven't stopped since. My journals from the last few years fill up notebook after notebook.

I write every day. Every morning. It's the first thing I do – well, the first thing once I've made a cup of tea. I write when insights occur to me too, or when something special happens that I want to remember. I write when I am feeling lonely, desperate, anxious or afraid and there is no-one to turn to. In other words, my journal almost becomes a person itself – it's someone to whom I can tell all my thoughts.

Apparently most people feel, as I do, that when they are writing a journal it's as if they are talking to someone else, even though it's highly unlikely that anyone else will actually read their writing. In fact, I wouldn't want anyone to read my journals, yet I still feel like I am writing to someone.

I write when I'm alone at home. I write when I'm away from home and in a strange place feeling lonely. One of my pet hates is eating alone in cafes and restaurants. I worry that everyone else is looking at me, thinking how pathetic I am that I have no friends to dine with. Even hiding behind the pages of a good novel does not alleviate this feeling. But bringing my journal and writing a few thoughts as I enjoy a meal *does*. I imagine I look like JK Rowling, penning the first Harry Potter in a coffee shop in Edinburgh. I don't need a fellow diner. My journal almost becomes my dining companion. (Though I admit that this isn't very mindful – see Idea 23.)

Sometimes, when life feels empty, having something to write isn't very easy. If I've got up every morning and done the same boring job that I've done the day before and the day before that, and then sat home alone every evening, watching TV, I don't generally find that I've much to say in the pages of a journal. What do you write? "Get up, had shower, got dressed, cornflakes for breakfast…."

One of the best books I ever bought helped with this. *The Artist's Way* by Julia Cameron was really written as a creative course to help writers struggling with writers' block. For me it was much more. It was almost like therapy. And it took my journaling to a different level. Every morning, you write 3 pages – morning pages as Julia Cameron calls them – before you do anything else. I have written morning pages for several years now. But *The Artists Way* does much more than encourage you to write. It encourages you to look at the world around you and at your own life in more detail – to realise that all the pebbles on the beach, for example, are all different or to think about who you were as an 8 year old child, what your hopes and dreams were. The book stimulated my imagination and suddenly I found that I had lots to say in my journal.

Journaling for me is first and foremost a safe way to express my inner thoughts and feelings, especially when I feel alone and have no-one to turn to. Rather than repressing my feelings, rather than bottling everything up, I can write everything down, let everything out.

Releasing myself from loneliness is, for me, all about making connections. The connection in the case of journalising is not to another person or to a higher power but to myself, to my innermost self. Sometimes that inner self remains hidden, even to me, because of the pressure to perform at work or to function socially. Journaling allows me to connect to that hidden inner self. It helps me to find my authentic self and allows me, quite simply, to be me.

Idea 10: Get creative

Why should we all use our creative power....? Because there is nothing that makes people so generous, joyful, lively, bold and compassionate, so indifferent to fighting and the accumulation of objects and money.
~ Brenda Ueland

Think of some of the great creative geniuses in history, and you'll find yourself naming some of the great loners too. There's a definite link between loneliness and creativity. In *Solitude*, psychiatrist and author Anthony Storr argues that the modern age overvalues personal relationships and that "many of the world's greatest thinkers have not reared families or formed close personal ties. This is true of Descartes, Newton, Locke, Pascal, Spinoza, Kant, Leibniz, Schopenhauer, Nietzsche, Kierkegaard and Wittgenstein ....none of them married and most lived alone for the greater part of their lives." So throughout the centuries, artists, religious figures, writers, political thinkers, and philosophers have valued being alone, rather than experiencing it as a cause of suffering. "My art takes birth when my loneliness becomes my companion," states the contemporary artist Jeet Aulakh.

Solitude might lead to creativity, but could the reverse be true? Could creativity be an answer to loneliness?

My experience tells me yes. When I turn off the TV (see Idea 8) and find something else to do, I find myself in the kitchen baking a cake or writing my journal or even painting a picture. I find myself doing creative things.

The Hungarian psychology professor, Mihály Csíkszentmihályi, who I've already mentioned in Idea 8, coined the term "flow" to describe the state of feeling fully absorbed in what you are doing. More engaging activities take you over some kind of threshold – activities that involve your active participation rather than just sitting passively on the sofa with your eyes glued to that square box. Getting creative is just one way of finding something more active to do.

Keeping a journal and reading *The Artists Way* by Julia Cameron really sparked my creativity. I'd estimate that 70% of my creativity revolves around writing – I've started writing (but not finishing) various books and I write several blogs. 29% revolves around eating – well, the creative part is the cooking but I'm motivated to do it because I like eating! The remaining 1% is various little projects that I start (though again, I often don't finish) such as decorating a room, painting a canvas, doing a collage or simply putting my photo collection into albums.

Never mind Kirstie Allsopp and her homemade home - I've sewed things, made hand-crafted cards, knitted (unwearable) jumpers, made those fancy cupcakes that are so trendy at the moment and filled the mantelpiece with glass-painted jam jars containing tea-lights. I've even been to classes on collage and using fabrics. Next on the list is revamping the dining room and learning to cook all the sorts of things that I like to eat in restaurants but never know how to make at home like peppercorn sauce and potato rosti.

If I'm lacking inspiration, a browse round the creative section of the local bookstore (or even just on Amazon) usually gives me a few ideas, as do the websites *Not on the High Street* and *Etsy*. If I'm still stuck for ideas, I look at *Living Out Loud: An Activity Book to Fuel a Creative Life* by Keri Smith or even go to the website Groupon for courses in everything from chocolate making to photography.

When I first started on trying to be creative and was working my way through *The Artists Way*, I felt a bit stupid making a collage. Cutting and sticking were things that I felt were more appropriate for someone aged 4, not someone aged 42. But I stuck with it and was soon experiencing that mysterious sense of flow. I was engaged in my collage: the hours and minutes flew by. Loneliness and his best buddy boredom disappeared.

Idea 11: Learn to enjoy solitude

The wisdom of our language has sensed....two sides of man's being alone. It has created the word 'loneliness' in order to emphasize the pain of being alone. And it has created the word 'solitude' in order to emphasize the glory of being alone. In daily life, these words are not always distinguished; but we should do so consistently, thus deepening the understanding of our human predicament.
~ Paul Tillich, philosopher

Once, for a TV programme I was making, I interviewed Michael Perham, who in 2009, had just become the youngest person to sail single-handedly around the world, aged just 17. For the purposes of the programme, I asked him all the questions I was supposed to ask: what made him decide to go? Was it difficult? What hardships did he have to endure? What kept him going? Once the cameras stopped rolling, I asked him the question I was desperate to know the answer to: "Weren't you lonely?"

He wasn't, he told me. I suppose Michael, at the tender age of 17, had already learnt something that I hadn't. He'd learnt to enjoy solitude. He experienced being alone as solitude, as a positive experience, not as loneliness.

I was jealous. It's become so trendy to go off and do something on your own. People go off to undertake physical challenges like climbing Everest or sailing around the world like Michael. I once interviewed a chap for *The Heaven and Earth Show* on BBC who had opted out of living in a conventional house and was sleeping rough in the woods in Oxfordshire all by himself. He loved it. Mark Boyle, the author of *The Moneyless Man*, did a similar thing, going to live by himself in the countryside in a caravan, without money for an entire year. Then there's the spiritual option – people go off to ashrams for months on end, like Elizabeth Gilbert does in the book *Eat Pray Love*.

I know all this is supposed to lead to personal growth. I wish I had the courage to try it. But, as Emily

White says in her book *Lonely: A Memoir*, "A different sort of dialogue attaches itself to aloneness that hasn't been chosen. Someone sitting alone at the foot of Everest blogs about his experience. Someone sitting alone in her living room night after night keeps the experience to herself."

A friend once gave me a book called *Succulent Women* by a writer known simply as Sark. As I read, I realised that I was not what you'd call a "succulent woman" – I was what Sark referred to as a "captive woman". Captive women, says Sark, "never go out without a man, or a group of women. If questioned about going out alone, they make squeamish faces and say, 'I couldn't go out *alone*. It wouldn't be any fun.' Even women who are not like this are shy about going out alone. There is still a social stigma about being out 'alone' (translation: boring, desperate, nobody likes her). Going out alone is a skill and an art that can be learned, shared and implemented."

I think staying in alone is a skill that can be learned too. As a self-employed person, working in a creative industry, I'm used to spending much of my time alone and some of the time, I actually like it. That, for me, is solitude. But, as Emily White has pointed out, choosing to be alone is quite different from having loneliness forced upon you. It's a different thing altogether on New Year's Eve when I've no-one to kiss to say "Happy New Year" or on a Saturday night when all of my friends are busy and I've nowhere to go and no-one to go out with. It's a different thing when my diary is much emptier than I'd like it to be or no-one has emailed me on internet dating. At times like that, I feel that I have no choice but to be alone and it ceases to be a nice feeling.

According to Rae Andre, author of *Positive Solitude*, when you're feeling lonely, it's because you're experiencing a "feedback gap". When I had just got divorced, I suddenly found myself coming home to an empty house, eating dinner alone and having no warm body to snuggle up to in bed. Putting the TV on as soon as I got in, eating my dinner watching it and buying an electric blanket were poor substitutes for human company.

"Among those who believe that being alone can be a positive experience, a common theme is that a person alone must be able to provide his or her own feedback," says Andre. "If you live alone in environments that reinforce your fear, tension, and anger, you will be unhappy; if you live alone in environments that reinforce relaxation, creativity, and happiness, you will be content."

Making my environment feel safe was crucial to learning to enjoy aloneness, experiencing the pleasure of solitude rather than the angst of loneliness. Just after my husband left, I took one of my first steps towards this, when I had a burglar alarm fitted with a panic button upstairs next to my bed. I never needed to use it but it gave me a feeling of safety and that immediately made living alone a bit easier. I was able to relax in bed at night, despite being completely unaccustomed to sleeping on my own.

The move from loneliness to solitude is a difficult one. The Catholic priest and psychologist Henri Nouwen writes:

> ...what then can we do with our essential aloneness which so often breaks into our consciousness as the experience of a desperate sense of loneliness? What does it mean to say that neither friendship nor love, neither marriage nor community can take that loneliness away? Sometimes illusions are more livable than realities, and why not follow our desire to cry out in loneliness and search for someone whom we can embrace and in whose arms our tense body and mind can find a moment of deep rest and enjoy the momentary experience of being understood and accepted? These are hard questions because they come forth out of our wounded hearts, but they have to be listened to even when they lead to a difficult road. This difficult road is the road of conversion, the conversion from loneliness into solitude. Instead of running away from our

53

loneliness and trying to forget it or deny it, we have to protect it and turn it into a fruitful solitude. To live a spiritual life we must first find the courage to enter into the desert of our loneliness and to change it by gentle and persistent efforts into a garden of solitude.

But, he continues, "Our world ... is not divided between lonely people and solitaries. We constantly fluctuate between these poles and differ from hour to hour, day to day, week to week and year to year."

One of the keys to unlocking the door of our loneliness and entering into a world of solitude, where the physical state of being alone can be a productive state, rather than a destructive one, seems to be discovering one's inner voice.

"The development of ... inner sensitivity," says Nouwen, "is the beginning of a spiritual life. It seems that the emphasis on interpersonal sensitivity that helps us to listen to our own inner voices. Sometimes one wonders if the fact that so many people ask support, advice and counsel from so many other people is not, in large part, due to their having lost contact with their innermost self."

When I first separated from my ex-husband, I tried to run away from my loneliness. I filled the silent house with noise from the TV. I filled my empty days with a whirl of social engagements – dates from the internet, drinks with colleagues, all manner of classes and evening activities. I did not want to be alone. I did not want to endure silence. I completely drowned out my inner voice and I lost contact with my innermost self.

But running away from something doesn't make that something go away. No matter how busy I was, my loneliness still lurked, driving me to make the next date or join the next social club. It was always there, reminding me that it was waiting for me at home, so I tried to go home as little as possible.

In her book *Shortcuts to Bouncing Back from Heartbreak*, author Gael Lindenfeld advocates having two periods of positive solitude each week doing something that is a treat, like reading the Sunday papers in Starbucks or going to an art gallery. The idea is to get used to being alone in a positive way, so that spending time alone is no longer something to be feared.

Once I settled down to this, once I turned the TV off occasionally and spent the odd weekend home alone, baking cakes and cooking soups for the freezer and doing other things I enjoyed doing, I started to feel more at ease with myself. Often, I was still lonely. Sometimes, I had glimpses of solitude, of real joy at spending time at home with no-one to please but myself. That joy, that "garden of solitude" as Henri Nouwen calls it, was there all the time, waiting to be discovered. But it was only when I stopped running and allowed myself to be still that I found it.

Idea 12: Deal with your other fears

I learned that courage was not the absence of fear, but the triumph over it. The brave man is not he who does not feel afraid, but he who conquers that fear.
~ Nelson Mandela

I experienced one of my loneliest times recently. I'd rented a cottage and gone away for a week on my own. It was a cottage I had stayed at before. I wasn't afraid of being alone there – on the contrary, I was looking forward to it. I was looking forward to having time to walk, read, write and perhaps do some art.

After a long journey, my most pressing need when I arrived at the cottage was to go to the toilet. I dashed in, sat down, looked up and saw, to my horror, right above the door and only a couple of feet away from me, an absolutely enormous spider. I am terrified of spiders. Somehow, I managed to leave the toilet, convinced as I was that the spider would cunningly drop down onto me to give me a fright as I walked underneath it.

I know it's illogical. I know that spiders don't have on their 'to do' list "Frighten humans". I know that to that spider I am a big enormous thing that he'd rather stay away from. But knowing that it's illogical just doesn't change how I feel.

I knocked on the neighbour's door and a woman answered. I explained the problem. She said that she used to be scared of spiders too but had overcome her fears and learnt to "deal with" them. She came over, confidently striding through the front door and straight up the stairs into the bathroom. When she saw the size and position of the spider, her confidence evaporated and she seemed a bit less certain about being able to deal with him. But she plucked up courage and soon the spider was no more.

"I'm afraid there'll be lots of spiders," she told me. "The cottages are full of them."

"But I've stayed here before," I said, "I didn't see any." She explained that it was the time of year. When I'd first stayed, it had been winter. Not a spider in sight. Now it was late summer and they were all coming inside.

Suddenly my holiday cottage changed from being a safe haven where I could do my writing to being a place where I had to endure spending the night alone. I just didn't feel comfortable there. I didn't feel safe there. I didn't want to sit on the sofa and read or sit at the little desk in my bedroom, writing and admiring the view, because I was scared that something might crawl across my foot. I didn't even enjoy my morning cuppa in bed as I was constantly wondering if something was lurking behind the headboard.

During the day, I went walking, wandering around for hours, finding little places to have a cuppa and write my journal. I felt homeless somehow and very alone. I felt like I just had nowhere to go – I had nowhere where I felt safe anyhow. But the nights were the worst. They were so lonely. I couldn't sleep because I felt so on edge. I guess that the fear was making adrenaline pump through my veins. So I lay awake. There is nothing so lonely as lying awake whilst the rest of the world is sleeping. And there were, inevitably, more spiders. If I went to the loo in the night, there was invariably one in there. Or on the stairs. Or on the landing. And sometimes in my room.

I learnt to deal with them – with the back of a shoe – but my heart was permanently pounding. "Why," I asked myself, "aren't I on holiday with a nice man who would protect me from these scary creatures?" I felt the pain of being single. If I had someone to go on holiday with, I reasoned, this wouldn't be so difficult and I wouldn't be having such a rotten time.

It was a vicious circle. Having to deal on my own with something I was so afraid of – the spiders – made me feel more alone than ever. And that feeling of being so alone, so completely alone, made the spiders seem even more threatening.

In the cold light of day, back in my own spider free house, it seems ridiculous. But it was as if one fear fed into another, compounding it, making it bigger. Dealing with the spiders by myself made me feel a sharp ache of loneliness, a longing for another human being to help me, a yearning to be part of a couple, just to have someone else there to keep me safe.

The last straw came when one morning there were four large spiders lurking around the front door. There was no back door so that front door was the only way out. I was scared to go past these creatures so I felt like they were trapping me, holding me prisoner inside the cottage. Heart thumping, I managed to kill all of them. I know it's cruel. I hardly ever eat meat because I love animals, but I just was not brave enough to do the paper and cup technique and get rid of them more humanely. Instead of going out walking as I'd planned, when the spiders were gone, I went back to my room and packed my stuff. Then I left. I'd only managed 3 days of my week.

Of course, not everyone is scared of spiders, but I suspect that many of our fears, rational and irrational, feel much worse when we're alone and then they add to our feelings of loneliness. Fear of the dark, for example. Fear of crime. Fear of open spaces. Fear of enclosed spaces. Having to deal with something that we're frightened of is so much easier when we're with another human being, when we aren't having to cope on our own.

There's a simple biological reason for this. "Throughout evolution," says the report *The Lonely Society,* "social bonds have been essential to our survival." It seems we are pre-programmed to feel safer in groups because, on the plains of Africa, many millennia ago, our ancestors were safer in groups. A threat was less of a threat to them if they were with other people, protecting each other.

I feel more terrified by that spider when I am alone than when I am with someone, but it helps to understand that feeling as a simple, biological response to something that makes me feel threatened. If I'm with other people, and an 8-legged beastie comes crawling along the floor, I'm scared. If I'm on my own, I feel not only my fear, but a sense of loneliness as well. I simply don't want to deal with the object of my fear by myself. The spider triggers my loneliness.

I don't believe that I can ever remove loneliness from my life completely but I can look at some of the things that trigger it and try to avoid them, just as an allergy sufferer might avoid eating nuts or shellfish or whatever triggers their allergy. But I knew that I couldn't avoid spiders forever. Even if I never saw another spider in my life, my fear would still be there. Every time I went to stay somewhere new on my own, I'd be wondering: will there be spiders there? Then I'd be wishing I was with someone. Then I'd be feeling lonely because I had no-one. So my only option was to deal with my fear. I booked myself on a therapy programme at a nearby zoo.

A few weeks later, I was standing with a live, poisonous and particularly hairy tarantula sitting in the palm of my hand. I even allowed the tarantula to crawl up my bare arm a little bit before asking for it to be removed. My loneliness did not evaporate at that moment. My fear of spiders didn't evaporate either. Not completely. But it was a start. I realised that I could accept my fear and still deal with the thing that I was frightened of. I realised that I needn't be dominated by my fear: I could face up to it. The connection between my fear and my loneliness seemed weakened somehow.

This is about connecting with my inner self. Deep within me, I have always had this fear of spiders. It's a part of me. 99% of the time I don't see many spiders. It's only when I'm gardening or I go on holiday somewhere tropical or we have a particularly wet autumn and they all come into the house seeking sanctuary. The rest of the time, I manage to forget my fear, to deny its existence. Going on the fear of spiders workshop allowed me not just to face up to my 8-legged friends, to confront them in a safe environment, but also to connect with that inner part of me, that fear that always resides within me, even when I pretend that it isn't there.

Whatever your fear, if it triggers your loneliness (and even, it might be argued, if it doesn't) it might be worth getting some help to deal with it. I do find it really empowering that very soon, I'll be able to deal with spiders on my own, in a humane way, and they will no longer be able to trigger a fear response and make me feel lonely. Who knows, I might even grow to love the hairy little things and get a pet tarantula to keep me company on those long winter evenings.

Idea 13: Count your blessings

*The single greatest thing you can do to change your life today would be
to start being grateful for what you have right now.
And the more grateful you are, the more you get.*
~ Oprah Winfrey

Remember the *Making Slough Happy* programme that I
mentioned before? I decided early on in my quest to be less
lonely that rather than trying to be less lonely, I should try
to be more happy and one of the recommendations in
Making Slough Happy was to cultivate a grateful attitude and
to say thank you to those people in your life to whom you
owe thanks. "Being aware of the good things in our lives
and expressing appreciation for them are some of the key
ways in which to be happy," according to Dr Richard
Stevens, the psychologist who headed up the team of
experts on the programme.

Psychologists and mental health practitioners agree
that expressing gratitude makes a significant difference to
levels of happiness. Chris Peterson, a psychology professor
at the University of Michigan, set his students the task of
writing a thank you letter to someone in their lives. After
the exercise, he found that his students felt happier.

In the TV programme, the participants were not
only asked to write a letter to someone: they had to meet
with that person and read it out to them, in public at a
special dinner. There were tears of joy all round.

But you don't have to say thank you *to* someone in
order to cultivate this appreciative attitude towards life. You
could just keep a diary, writing down all the things that have
gone well, all the things you feel grateful for. I think it might
have been Oprah Winfrey who started the trend for keeping
a blessings journal like this, a daily record of all the things
that have gone right for you in a day.

When I first tried this, I didn't feel particularly
grateful for anything and I didn't know what to write. I was

61

at a stage where I didn't feel anything good was really happening in my life. When I look back on my journals, I see that I chose easy things, very general things, like having had a nice dinner or having somewhere nice to live or even having had a particularly nice cup of tea. Someone smiling at me in the park and giving me a few words of encouragement on my daily run might make an entry. Getting a postcard from a friend on holiday or finding that my housemate had done all the washing up and I didn't need to bother. Once I got started, it became easier and easier to find things to be thankful for.

One of the big benefits of cultivating this attitude of gratitude was that it made me aware of what I had got rather than focusing all my attention on what I felt I was missing.

This might have made me feel happier, but could it actually help my loneliness?

When you keep a blessings diary, you'll begin to feel more connected to the world, according to the online publication, *Psychology Today*: "Call it corny, but gratitude just may be the glue that holds society together."

Apparently, when people are thanked for doing something good, they are more likely to do that action again in the future. So thanking someone has a knock-on effect: the more thanks there are going around, the more good deeds there are likely to be too. I make a point of thanking drivers who let me out into the queue of traffic: that way, they're much more likely to let other drivers out and if we all started that, driving would be a bit more pleasurable.

In the last ten years or so, there's been a lot of scientific research into the effect that gratitude has on people's well-being. Scientists have suggested that gratitude has one of the strongest links with well-being of almost any personality characteristic. Grateful people, it turns out, are less depressed, less stressed and much happier with their lives. They are also more satisfied with their social relationships which would seem to suggest that if you cultivate a thankful attitude, you are more likely to make meaningful connections with other people.

Grateful people are also more likely to seek support from other people when they encounter difficulties in life. Giving and receiving support is one of the ways in which people form bonds with other people, so being able to accept help from someone else is one way in which we'll feel more connected to others, thereby reducing our feelings of loneliness.

Idea 14: Get regular exercise

Lack of activity destroys the good condition of every human being, while movement and methodical physical exercise save it and preserve it.
~ Plato

So now I'm not just focusing on getting rid of my loneliness, but on increasing my levels of happiness and it's a well-known fact that exercise doesn't just bring physical benefits – it has an effect on emotional well-being too.

According to the Gallup-Healthways Well-Being Index, in which Gallup analyzed the results of more than 400,000 interviews, conducted from May 2008 to April 2009, those who exercise at least two days per week report experiencing more happiness and less stress than those who do not.

Exercise improves your mood, decreases your levels of stress and anxiety and can even raise self-confidence.

Apparently it's because of hormones called endorphins. When you exercise, these hormones are released in your brain and they are responsible for enhancing your mood.

So I donned my running shoes, reluctantly at first. I was motivated by a desire to feel better and also, if I'm honest, to lose a few pounds into the bargain. Well, actually, the first step was *buying* running shoes. I didn't own a single pair of anything that resembled a trainer.

Given that I was the world's *least* sporty person at school – our PE teacher somewhat cruelly dubbed me "Weed of the Week" – it was quite a shock to suddenly find myself wanting to exercise. Well, I say wanting … but in reality, it was an ordeal at first. I started off running for one minute, and walking for three, and I repeated that 8 times per session. Initially, I was exhausted after the first minute and only just got my breath back after three minutes of walking in time to start the running bit again. I couldn't imagine that I was *ever* going to be able to run for a whole 30 minutes or more without stopping.

But I did. I built up gradually. Running for two minutes, walking for two minutes. Running for three minutes. Walking for two minutes. Eventually, I ran for ten minutes, had a break then did another ten minutes. Then one day, I just kept going. I run about ten kilometres now and I love it.

Does it improve my loneliness? Yes, it does. Because it's something that I can do on my own. When I'm feeling miserable and bored and those feelings of loneliness are threatening to kick in, I put on my running shoes, get out in the fresh air and let the endorphins kick in instead.

I run alone, but exercise provides plenty of opportunities for socialising. I'm not really into gyms, though I know people who've made friends there and even found boyfriends. But I have been to my local running club and my local Pilates class and both were friendly, sociable places that I'd go to more regularly if I had more time. Sometimes, running is a bit too energetic so I've been out on group rambles and they're both good exercise and sociable. There's plenty of walking groups about too: take a look at the Ramblers Association website, and look for a local group that has social events like meeting in the pub for a drink, as well as rambles.

So there are two good reasons to start exercising if you feel lonely: those mood-enhancing hormones and the socializing opportunities that exercising with other people brings. But there's another reason why I started: blood pressure.

I've always had normal blood pressure – at the low end of the normal range in fact. But then suddenly, I was told that my blood pressure was a bit high and getting more exercise seemed a good way of doing something about that. After all, I didn't want to have to put less salt on my chips!

Does blood pressure have anything to do with loneliness? Apparently so. Researchers at the University of Chicago discovered that there is a direct relationship between loneliness and increases in blood pressure. They studied over 200 people between the ages of 50 to 68 and discovered that blood pressure appears to rise after four years of loneliness.

"Loneliness behaved as though it is a unique health-risk factor in its own right," wrote researcher Louise Hawkley in an article, "Loneliness Predicts Increased Blood Pressure," published in the journal *Psychology and Aging*.

This fact hit the headlines in the UK in February 2012, with the Daily Mail reporting that the "Elderly should get a job to combat loneliness and help them live longer".

According to the paper, a Downing Street adviser said "Pensioners should go back to work because loneliness is more deadly than smoking…David Halpern claimed that strong social relationships in the workplace would help people to live longer."

The reason for this is simple. According to *The Lonely Society,* if our expectations of our relationships are not being met, "our body starts to alert us that something is wrong: we feel physically threatened." This perception of a physical threat makes us feel stress. When someone feels stressed, their body produces a hormone called cortisol. Cortisol causes the level of sugar in the blood to rise and suppresses the immune system. It's part of the body's natural response to a stressful situation. But when stress is suffered more frequently, over a longer period of time, the result of all this cortisol can have harmful effects on health, causing high blood pressure, for example, and possibly weakening your immune system.

The good news is that the endorphins produced when we exercise should moderate the detrimental effects of this prolonged release of cortisol. (Actually, cortisol is released when you exercise too, but it's the prolonged exposure to it in response to feeling stressed and/or lonely that has such a negative effect on your health).

I tend to be the sort of person who starts something, does it for a while then gives up. I'm rather surprised that I've kept up with my running regime over the last couple of years. But the benefits are so tangible that it's impossible not to. My blood pressure has gone down, I look a bit slimmer and those mood-enhancing hormones really lift my spirits when my loneliness is getting me down.

Idea 15: Stop seeing yourself as the problem

If we can really understand the problem, the answer will come out of it, because the answer is not separate from the problem.
~ Jiddu Krishnamurti

As I read more about loneliness, the more I realised that this problem was bigger than just me. I realised, as I described in Idea 1, that I was not alone. But I also realised that loneliness wasn't just a common problem that a lot of us experience because we lack friends or a life partner. It goes far beyond that.

The causes of my loneliness go far beyond me not having met Mr Right. They're tied up with the way our society is structured today, the ways in which our communities are breaking down and the ways in which our working lives are changing.

"No-one is left from the Glenn Valley, Pennsylvania, Bridge Club, who can tell us precisely when or why the group broke up," says Robert Putnam in *Bowling Alone*, "even though its forty-odd members were still playing regularly as recently as 1990, just as they had done for more than half a century. The shock in the Little Rock, Arkansas, Sertoma club, however, is still painful: in the mid-1980s, nearly fifty people had attended the weekly luncheon to plan activities to help the hearing- and speech-impaired, but a decade later only seven regulars continued to show up.....Somehow in the last decades of the twentieth century all these community groups and tens of thousand like them across America began to fade."

"By virtually every conceivable measure," continues Putnam, "social capital has eroded steadily and sometimes dramatically over the past two generations. The quantitative evidence is overwhelming, yet most Americans did not need to see charts and graphs to know that something bad has been happening in their communities and in their country.

Americans have had a growing sense at some visceral level of disintegrating social bonds."

At the beginning of the 20th century, the average family was larger and more stable, divorce was much less common and comparatively few people lived on their own. As divorce became more common and family sizes decreased, there has been a huge rise in the number of single households. According to the Office for National Statistics, by 2011, 29 per cent of UK households consisted of only one person.

Modern cities have also been blamed for the rising rates of loneliness. Living in a city surrounded by millions of people when you don't feel a sense of connection to anyone can compound your feelings of isolation.

The Catholic priest and writer Henri Nouwen described a journey on the New York subway in his book, *Reaching Out:*

> I am surrounded by silent people hidden behind their newspapers or staring away in the world of their own fantasies. Nobody speaks with a stranger, and a patrolling policeman keeps reminding me that people are not out to help each other. But when my eyes wander over the walls of the train covered with invitations to buy more or new products, I see young, beautiful people enjoying each other in a gentle embrace, playful men and women smiling at each other on sailboats, proud explorers on horseback encouraging each other to take brave risks….while…I am nervously aware where I keep my money, the words and images decorating my fearful world speak about love, gentleness, tenderness and that joyful togetherness of spontaneous people. The contemporary society in which we find ourselves makes us acutely aware of our loneliness.

Like Nouwen, I see images all around me that point towards "togetherness". Sofa adverts on TV show families snuggling up cosily. A kitchen advert shows people having a fantastic time at a party. The brochure for a nearby housing development shows a couple proudly clinking glasses to celebrate their new home. Yet I'm on my own, feeling lonely. Am I abnormal? Or are the adverts simply glossing over the loneliness of modern life? Perhaps, I wonder cynically, they're exploiting our loneliness, making us believe that if we buy that kitchen and that sofa and a flat in that development, we'll start to feel better. I'm not sure I believe that, but I flick through the Ikea catalogue all the same.

Those sofa adverts, promoting togetherness as such an easily-achievable norm, make me feel abnormal but I'm not. If I've learnt anything from all the books I've read, it's that loneliness is a normal feeling. There's safety in numbers so we're pre-programmed to want to be near other people. As I've already mentioned, this drive to be near others would have helped our early ancestors to survive. But modern society – with its high-rise cities, its long working hours that leave people too tired to socialise, its emphasis on electronic communication rather than face-to-face interaction, its high divorce rates and single households – causes us to live in ways that undermine our sense of community.

I find it comforting to realise that my feelings of loneliness are not just caused by a failing on my part, but by a normal human reaction to the circumstances in which I find myself. Those circumstances too are not of my own making. Had I been around 100 years ago, I might not have got divorced so I wouldn't have been living alone. I'd have had children. If I'd gone out to work, I'd have had a conventional job rather than working from home on a freelance basis. In other words, I'm part of a bigger picture – a picture where the changes in the way we live and work leave us more vulnerable to feelings of loneliness and isolation.

Idea 16: Write a list of things to do

Boredom: the desire for desires.
~ Leo Tolstoy

My loneliness hardly ever strikes me on its own. It almost always comes hand in hand with its best buddy boredom, and together, they whack me over the head with a mallet and render me incapable of doing anything other than watching *Come Dine with Me* and other such programmes on the TV. Entertaining though those programmes might be, they don't really make me feel any better, but the longer I watch, the less inclined I am to get up off the sofa and do something about my loneliness and boredom.

According to psychiatrists Jacqueline Olds and Richard Schwartz, "Everyone, no matter what their psychological background, becomes worried and fretful and feels insecure in the face of large amounts of unscheduled time….It is true that being with someone else often has a mind-focusing effect that makes fretfulness a little less likely, but it is also possible to reduce the anxiety and sadness associated with loneliness by yourself. This can be achieved by cultivating a repertoire of "flow" activities, which so strongly engage your creativity that you become oblivious to the passage of time."

One way I achieve "flow" is by going for a run (see Idea No. 14). Getting some exercise almost always raises me out of my slump and makes me feel better. I also find "flow" by being creative (see Idea 10) but the trouble is, when I feel bored, lonely and completely fed up, my imagination seems to disappear and I can't think of anything that I *want* to do. The solution, I've found, is to keep a list of things to do when I'm feeling bored. I look upon it like a menu in a restaurant. I suppose this is what Olds and Schwartz mean when they say a "repertoire of 'flow' activities". I can select from my repertoire – or my "bored list" as I like to call it – and do whatever I want from that list, but I *have* to select something. Sometimes, I really have to force myself to select something.

The list consists mostly of things that are either fun or useful or both. It might be looking through my old collection of VHS tapes and transferring one or two to DVD. It might be going through my wardrobe and finding 5 things I no longer wear that can be given to charity. It might be making a few birthday cards so I've something to send when friends' birthdays come round. It might be re-designing my website or making a cake or re-organising the kitchen cupboards and getting rid of out of date foods.

The internet is full of lists like mine – lists other people have compiled of things to do when you're bored. Some of them consist of silly things: race ferrets, build a pyramid or pretend you're a robot. Others suggest more productive activities like researching your family tree online, going to an art gallery or making your own video for Youtube. The good thing about compiling my own list, rather than relying on other people's, is that I've made sure that it consists of things that I like doing and things that give me "flow". Doing those things makes me feel productive, thereby lifting me from my bad mood.

I've made a new version of my list recently: it's a card version. I used Google images to find pictures representing most of the activities on my bored list. Then I printed them out onto card, so they were all the same size, cut them out and put them through a laminator. If I'm feeling so bored and fed up that I don't have the energy to choose something from my list, I just pick a card at random. It sounds silly, but it works.

Idea 17: Do things you enjoyed as a child

In every real man a child is hidden that wants to play.
~ Friedrich Wilhelm Nietzsche

Loneliness, as I've already mentioned, seldom knocks on my door without being accompanied by his chum boredom. The only way out of this seems to be to fill my time with activities that feel meaningful and that I enjoy doing, but when I'm in that deep rut of loneliness, it's difficult to think of what those activities might be. I've already suggested "getting creative" (Idea 10) and "keeping a journal" (Idea 9) In Idea 16, I explored the idea of keeping a list of things to do when you're bored, so you can choose from it like a kind of menu. But sometimes, it's hard to think of things to put on that list.

"Take time out to remember what you *used* to like," advises Rae Andre in *Positive Solitude*. "What were your consistently favourite activities as a child?"

Re-visiting your childhood hobbies is also explored by author Gretchen Rubin in her book *The Happiness Project*. Gretchen spent a whole year devoting herself to researching happiness and trying to raise her own levels of happiness. In May of that year, her goal was to have more fun:

> I told a friend that I was trying to have more fun, and instead of pointing me toward the 'Going On About Town' column in *The New Yorker,* she asked me a question: 'What did you like to do when you were a child? What you enjoyed as a ten-year-old is probably something you'd enjoy now.'
>
> That was an intriguing idea. I remembered that Carl Jung, when he was thirty-eight years old, had decided to start playing with building blocks again, to tap into the enthusiasm he'd felt as an eleven-year old. What had I done for fun as a child? No

chess, no ice-skating, no painting. I worked on my 'Blank Books'.

Gretchen describes how she had been given a blank notebook by an uncle as a birthday present and how this had led her to keep a whole collection of blank books. They'd been filled with clippings, notes from school friends, cartoons – basically anything that interested her.

When I read Gretchen's description of her blank books, it reminded me of the books that *I* used to keep as a child. Often they were school projects, compiled in big scrapbooks, but I'd go above and beyond the requirements of school and spend hours working on them. Sometimes I'd keep my own scrapbook record of a holiday. I wrote novels and short stories too.

I've started writing novels again now. They aren't very good and I'm pretty sure that I'm not the next JK Rowling. It doesn't matter if no-one ever reads them and they don't bring anyone any pleasure - just writing them brings *me* pleasure. I have learnt to let go of the idea that it's the finished product that's important – it is the act of producing that is key here. I've started keeping my scrapbooks again too, albeit in a small way. I have a small scrapbook detailing the key points from any book I read and like, with a small picture of the front cover of each book stuck in for good measure.

Another activity that I enjoyed as a child was watching ballet. I loved ballet. I know this isn't typical teenage behaviour and will probably make me sound a little strange (you'll be thinking – aha! I know why *she's* lonely!) But as a teenager, whenever I was left alone in the house, I'd watch my collection of ballet videos. Over and over again.

I still have them. They hadn't been looked at for ages, but recently, when I was considering what things I could do now that I enjoyed as a child, I got them out again. I didn't fancy anything that involved getting in a swimming costume and horse-riding makes me sneeze these days. But watching the videos and transferring them from VHS to

DVD is great fun. It doesn't involve getting wet hair *or* smelling of horse.

Once I get started on this activity or on my "blank books", the hours pass and I forget about my boredom. And my loneliness.

Idea 18: Plan for difficult times and situations

Christmas is a holiday that persecutes the lonely,
the frayed, and the rejected.
~ Jimmy Cannon

After more than 7 years as a divorced woman and a lot of time thinking about my life and how I want to live it, I feel like I am well on the way to being happy again and I hardly ever feel lonely these days.

But there are still a few occasions. Every year, as July gets closer, I wonder if anyone will invite me out for my birthday. Will anyone buy me gifts? Make me feel special? On Bank Holidays, I hope my friends will be free to do something. I hate being home alone with no plans at all on a Saturday night too. But Christmas is by far the worst time: Christmas is the time when I feel that I should have a family to cook for, I should have children to buy presents for and hang up stockings for and I should have a partner to buy something nice for who'll buy me something nice in return. I don't actually spend Christmas alone: I have my very wonderful parents and my sister who's a chef and always cooks a great turkey. But it's just not what I expected to be doing on Christmas Day at the ripe old age of 42. I thought I'd have a family of my own by now.

In *Positive Solitude,* Rae Andre suggests making an inventory of the times when you feel lonely, bored or excluded. Christmas would definitely top my list. Once you've made that list, you can plan for it.

This year, Christmas was looming and my diary was empty. I was dreading it. I was having Christmas lunch with my parents as usual but had absolutely nothing else planned for the entire week of Christmas and New Year. My housemate, who is also my best friend, was going home to see *his* parents for almost a week and I foresaw several days of loneliness and boredom over the festive season. I nearly didn't tell my friends, for fear that they'd all already have plans and I'd not only feel bored and lonely, but rejected too. But in the end, I plucked up courage and sent a variety of messages on Facebook and by text, asking people what they were doing over Christmas and New Year. Did anyone fancy meeting up? I asked.

I got some knock-backs. Inevitably, there were people who were more organised than me and had every spare minute over Christmas and New Year already accounted for. But I got lots of invitations too. My sister invited me out for drinks on Christmas Eve and treated me to a bottle of champagne in the local pub. My friends Clare and Nige included me in their family gathering on Boxing Day: parents, in-laws, parents of in-laws, and children. I was the only non-family member but I felt included and it was lovely. I met other friends for lunch or drinks and invited a male friend over for a romantic candle-lit dinner.

By New Year's Eve, I was actually too exhausted to go out, but my housemate was back home by then so we saw the New Year in quietly together.

I could have resignedly accepted a lonely Christmas but I didn't. Knowing that it's a difficult time for me, I planned things to do and it worked. It was the best Christmas I've had in about a decade. Definitely the best I've had since I've been single.

I know there are people who aren't so lucky, who don't have a family that they can go to for Christmas lunch and who don't have so many friends. But there are still things you can do, rather than sitting home feeling miserable. I googled City Socialising and Meetup before Christmas looking for things to do and there were loads of things in my local area, that I could have fallen back on, if I'd needed to.

One of my friends takes herself off to Bali every Christmas on a yoga retreat. Another friend went on an organised holiday with the social group Spice over the festive season. One year, I plan on doing the same: perhaps booking a holiday with a company like Exodus or Explore where many of my fellow travellers are likely to be single like me. There's volunteering opportunities during

December too. One friend of mine always volunteers at the local homeless centre over Christmas and finds it very rewarding, and another friend gave it a try this year.

And it's not so bad if you do end up home alone. I had lunch with my parents one Christmas then headed home straight afterwards, just to prove to myself that I could survive Christmas afternoon and evening on my own. I did survive. I planned what I was going to watch. I made sure I had some treats in to eat.

When Radio 4's *You and Yours* did a phone in on loneliness just before Christmas 2010, a woman from Cheshire phoned in to tell the story of her Christmas alone, the previous year. She'd bought the boxed set of the original version of *Upstairs Downstairs* and spent the whole of Christmas Day and Boxing Day in bed watching it. She'd got picnic food to eat and only got up to go to the toilet and to replenish the picnic. She told her story with sheer delight: she'd clearly enjoyed herself.

The key seems to be in planning ahead. If I'm going to be alone at a time when I know I'll find it difficult, I need to stock up on those special foods that will make it feel special and buy that DVD boxed set. Though personally, I'd prefer *Downton Abbey* to *Upstairs Downstairs* any day.

Idea 19: Create solace

Writing is the supreme solace.
~ W. Somerset Maugham

When I was little, like many children, I had a security blanket. It was pale blue and woolly, but it had a satin edge that I liked to stroke. It gave me a feeling of comfort. Just like the character Linus in the comic strip Peanuts, I took my security blanket everywhere with me.

In the Peanuts cartoons, Linus gets relentlessly teased about his security blanket by Lucy, another of the characters. But psychiatrist Dr Paul Horton, author of *Solace: The Missing Dimension in Psychiatry*, says that people shouldn't be embarrassed about their need for a security blanket. We should just realise that we have one and enjoy it, whatever form it takes.

My journal is my security blanket these days (see Idea 9: Keep a journal). If I'm away from home and feeling lonely, I seek sanctuary in a coffee shop somewhere and wile away the hours writing and drinking lattes. But I do still have an *actual* blanket that brings me comfort. These days, I never leave the house with it: it's a beautiful, cream-coloured throw that usually lives on the sofa looking stylish but is great for cuddling up in when I'm feeling down or cold or both. It gives me a sense of solace.

The word solace comes from the Latin "sōlācium" and means comfort or consolation in a time of distress.

Objects that help us to find solace are termed "transitional objects" by psychologists. Donald Winnicott, an English paediatrician and psychoanalyst, first put forward the idea that a child's security blanket or soft toy might be a substitute for the feeling of security that the child would have in his or her mother's arms. Later research has shown that transitional objects might be necessary to our emotional development.

A transitional object is something that brings us a sense of solace. My journal and the cream throw on my sofa are my transitional objects. Charles Dickens' character David Copperfield had a book as his transitional object, whilst for French author Marcel Proust it was the taste of the little Madeleine cakes that he loved. According to Dr. Horton, a transitional object can be anything that triggers a "symbolic connection with an abiding, mainly maternal presence." A transitional object might not necessarily be a physical object: something simple like humming quietly brings comfort to some children. A piece of music, words from a poem or a special place to which we can retreat can all bring us that sense of comfort when we are struggling with our loneliness.

The best way of finding solace, says Dr. Horton, is to share your feelings with someone else. But if you're on your own, if you're lonely, by definition you don't have that someone else with whom you can share your feelings so you need to find a sense of solace some other way.

In Dr. Horton's research, other ways in which people find comfort include praying, reading, going for a walk and even talking to yourself. Recalling pleasant memories can also engender a sense of solace. "Recalling your first date with your spouse," says Dr. Horton, "can make you feel good during painful times." Hmmm….maybe I'll give that one a miss.

Ritual too can be a source of solace. In *The Complete Idiot's Guide to Motherhood*, author Deborah Herman advises those mothers struggling with the breakdown of a relationship to seek solace in ritual. This might be the ritual of a religious ceremony, for those who are so inclined, or it could be as simple as having a regular pizza night once a week or once a month.

Rae Andre, author of *Positive Solitude*, says that rituals can be an important source of solace because they "provide recurring connections to the past and to the future." "Rituals," says Andre, "also play a role in your everyday life. The way you rise in the morning, the way you work, the way you spend the twilight hours – all these acts may include solacing rituals….These rituals may be as simple as treating yourself to fried potatoes every Sunday morning or tending a garden every spring. Some of the rituals may be old family ones renewed; some may be of your own unique design. Whichever they may be, recognizing their contribution to the solace in your life is paramount."

One of my favourite types of solace is comfort food. On cold, wintry nights when the dark mornings and dark afternoons are getting us down, one of my friends and I have a well-established ritual: we go to the pub for egg, chips and beans. OK, it's not sophisticated fare, but we are both northerners.

When I'm home alone, I often seek solace in food. I don't mean that I sit stuffing my face with chocolate à la Vicar of Dibley (tempting though it is) but I cook myself a hot meal, something I find really delicious.

I thought that this was simply a case of me enjoying my food, but recently scientists have discovered that chicken soup really is good for the soul and, more to the point, comfort food actually helps fight loneliness.

In a study published in the journal *Psychological Science*, a journal of the Association for Psychological Science, Jordan Troisi and Shira Gabriel investigated social surrogates—non-human things which give people a sense of belonging.

In one experiment, researchers asked participants to write about a fight with someone close to them, in order to make them feel lonely. A control group was given an emotionally neutral writing assignment. Then, some people in each group wrote about eating a comfort food and others about eating a new food. All the participants then completed a questionnaire to assess their levels of loneliness. Those who had written about a comfort food seemed to "rescue themselves" from the loneliness that writing about a fight had triggered.

In another experiment, eating chicken soup in the lab made people think more about relationships, but only if they already considered chicken soup to be a comfort food.

"Throughout everyone's daily lives they experience stress, often associated with our connections with others," Troisi says. "Comfort food can serve as a ready-made, easy resource for remedying a sense of loneliness. Keeping in mind this new research, it seems humans can find a number of ways to feel like we're connected with others."

Time to open that can of baked beans and get the chip pan out....

Idea 20: Find meaning in your life

When Freud was asked what constituted psychological health, he gave as his answer the ability to love and work. We have over-emphasized the former and paid too little attention to the latter.
~ Anthony Storr, psychiatrist

I've been unemployed and single at the same time, and it's miserable. Whilst my friends and my housemate went off to their jobs, I was stuck home alone. They said they were too tired or too busy to meet in the evenings and I was left wondering what the point of my life was. Everyone else seemed to have a purpose. Except me. My life lacked meaning.

Perhaps this was a mid-life crisis. I'd given up my career working in television. I'd tried going back to primary school teaching and not enjoyed it. I didn't know what career I wanted to do (and I still don't!) I'd like to think there's a divine plan for me but I haven't a clue what it is

Last year, I was researching loneliness all day every day, in the run up to running a loneliness retreat at an abbey near Preston. I realized, as I researched, that I wasn't feeling lonely very much at all any more, but when a friend asked me what had changed, I couldn't figure it out.

As part of the research, I was ploughing through a huge pile of books I'd bought. One was Viktor Frankl's *Man's Search for Meaning*. I'd seen it in the "Mind, Body, Spirit" section of a local bookshop and been attracted by the colourful bird on the front cover.

Viktor Frankl was a psychiatrist who was interned in a Nazi concentration camp in World War 2. He noticed that some people survived the same terrible conditions that killed other people and spent time observing and trying to work out what the difference was. What did those people have that enabled them to live whilst others didn't? The answer: purpose. They had a book they wanted to write, a career they wanted to pursue or a loved one they wanted to get back to. They lived for that purpose.

Purpose. It was staring me in the face all along - *that* was what had changed in my life. I don't know why I hadn't realized it before. There's even a song about purpose in my favourite musical, *Avenue Q*: "Purpose – it's that little flame, that lights a fire under your ass. Purpose – it keeps you going strong, like a car with a full tank of gas." Having to do all that research for the loneliness retreat was lighting a fire under *my* ass. Not only had it been taking up all my spare time, it had felt so absorbing, so worthwhile.

According to Viktor, people found purpose in one of three ways: the first way is through work. Viktor noticed that some of the people who survived the ordeal of the camp had work that they really yearned to accomplish in their life; the second way was through love – some people managed to hang on in there because they wanted to see their soulmate or their children again; and in the third way, according to Viktor, "Even the most helpless victim of a hopeless situation, facing a fate he cannot change, may rise above himself, may grow beyond himself and by doing so may change himself."

I'm not sure that being unemployed and single really constitutes, in my case at least, being a "helpless victim of a hopeless situation." But I'd tried to find work. I'd tried to find love. And both were eluding me.

One evening in the pub, a friend who happens also to be a life coach suggested that finding my purpose might not mean finding one specific job that gives my life meaning, but could be fulfilled through any number of jobs, projects or hobbies. I realised that preparing for the retreat had indeed brought a sense of purpose into my life. I began to look for other ways to find purpose, not restricting myself to thinking in terms of a career, but thinking in broader terms of things I could do, whether they were things that would generate income or not.

I realized that what I most wanted to do was to help other people in some way. A friend of mine suggested that I wrote a self-help book using the materials I'd compiled for the retreat. I also started a project called Help100, with the aim of helping 100 people in a life changing way and I used my film-making skills to make a video for a charity involved in aid work in Africa.

I'm creating my own meaning. At those times when my lack of work and my lack of a romantic partner make me feel that my life has no purpose, I create my own. I invent little projects for myself and I get stuck into them.

It might be as simple as sorting out the kitchen. I realized recently that we had food in our cupboards and freezer that we never, ever used. I'm not talking about cans of baked beans that get eaten up on a fairly regular basis and then replaced, but things like mung beans and desiccated coconut and 4 whole packets of sage and onion stuffing mix that just sit there, taking up space and never getting eaten. Neither my housemate or I liked the mung beans so, much as I hate wasting food, they ended up in the bin, along with an out-of-date packet of Angel Delight that neither of us would admit to buying, but which had somehow found its way into the back of our cupboard. But when I started baking bread to use up a big packet of bread flour, I discovered that I liked baking bread. Even better, I liked *eating* home-made bread. I discovered that desiccated coconut makes sponge cakes more moist and that stuffing mix makes great dumplings. Our cupboards are more organized now, I've expanded my repertoire of things I can cook and we saved a bit of money into the bargain. OK, so "She was good at clearing kitchen cupboards" isn't what I want written on my gravestone, but it was still a fun project and gave me a sense of purpose when I had no job.

Books like *The Artists Way, 10 Days To Great Self-Esteem, The Don't Sweat The Small Stuff Workbook* and *Calling In The One* are great too. Books that require you to participate, rather than just being a passive reader. Books that you work your way through over a period of weeks. I still sweat the small stuff sometimes, I don't seem to have managed to "call in the one", my self-esteem isn't always great and I'm certainly no artist but all of those books have been little projects for me that have brought meaning to an otherwise dull couple of months.

I still haven't found a permanent job but instead of spending day after day stuck at home feeling miserable, I spend my days writing and working on ideas for Help100. My days have purpose and meaning and I feel a lot less lonely as a result.

Idea 21: Slow down

It is not enough to be busy; so are the ants.
The question is: what are we busy about?
~ Henry David Thoreau

In my attempts to stave off loneliness, I've been very, very busy. You might not get that impression from my descriptions of being lonely, bored, unemployed and sitting around watching repeats of *Come Dine with Me*, but I've had periods where I've hardly sat still. I've arranged social events left, right and centre, joined clubs, taken up hobbies, taken on freelance work, joined committees, been to political meetings, anything in fact that would mean that I wasn't sitting on the sofa home alone. There have been months in my life where I've successfully avoided spending *any* time on my own at all in the hope that I wouldn't feel lonely.

Did these efforts work? No, they did not. In *The Lonely American,* psychiatrists Jacqueline Olds and Richard Schwartz describe a cycle of busyness that lonely people – like me – sometimes get themselves into: "staying busy to avoid seeming lonely and feeling lonely because there seems to be no time to cultivate relationships."

"When people treat busyness as a virtue," say Olds and Schwartz, "they step back from one another. They hesitate before visiting or calling or inviting someone over. They hesitate, and the moment passes….We risk becoming a nation in which everyone feels a little neglected, a little left out. And we will all feel that it has been done *to* us, not *by* us."

Were my efforts to be busy and stave off loneliness actually exacerbating my loneliness rather than making it better? It was time to try taking things a little more slowly.

Years ago, when I was a researcher on BBC1's *Heaven and Earth Show,* we interviewed author Carl Honoré for an item on mobile phones. If my memory serves me rightly, I don't think Carl had a mobile phone. If he did, he certainly didn't use it much and he wasn't addicted to it like I was to mine.

Carl talked about how some people can't sit still for two minutes without getting their phone out. You only have to look around a train carriage to see that this is true. On a recent journey in London, there were ten people in my carriage. Of them, only two (and I was one!) didn't have a mobile phone in their hand. One woman was using a phone and an iPod simultaneously and another was using not one but *two* mobile phones, one to make a call on and the other to send texts. These days, I use my mobile a lot less and I'm proud to say that I can sit in a bar whilst my friend goes to the ladies without the need to get my phone out. But at the time we interviewed Carl, I couldn't.

If a friend was late arriving, and I was sitting alone in a pub or restaurant, I would *always* get my phone out. I think that was to do with my loneliness. I wanted to show to the outside world that I wasn't a Billy-No-Mates. I might be sitting alone but I was sending and receiving texts. I did *know* people.

I knew it wasn't healthy to be so addicted to my phone, but I didn't know how to help it, and that short interview with Carl made a bit of an impression on me at the time. So when I was thinking about ways to slow down in my life, to see if that helped my feelings of loneliness, I turned to Carl's book, *In Praise of Slow*. According to Carl, we're all believers in the "go-faster gospel" of modern living. "The problem," he says, "is that our love of speed, our obsession with doing more and more in less and less time has gone too far; it has turned into an addiction, a kind of idolatry….Everything about urban life – the cacophony, the cars, the crowds, the consumerism – invites us to rush rather than relax, reflect or reach out to people."

I like that little phrase and I wonder if it might be a good motto for anyone trying to change their life and slow down: "Relax, reflect and reach out to people."

The trouble is, we all seem to be rushing everywhere, trying to cram too many things into too little time. Small wonder then, that when we bump into a friend or a neighbour on the street, we've little time to stand and chat. Those spontaneous conversations may seem insignificant but they help us to make connections within our local communities – they help us to feel socially embedded. When we're dashing around, juggling the long commute, long working hours, school run and social life, home becomes little more than a place to sleep and we lose that sense of belonging. And then we feel lonely. We never have time to do nothing: to just be.

According to Carl Honoré, "In this media-drenched, data-rich, channel-surfing, computer-gaming age, we have lost the art of doing nothing, of shutting out the background noise and distractions, of slowing down and simply being alone with our thoughts. Boredom – the word itself hardly existed 150 years ago – is a modern invention."

This interests me. My loneliness is often exacerbated by boredom. It's a bit chicken and egg – I'm not sure whether being bored triggers my feelings of loneliness or whether being lonely triggers my feelings of boredom. The two feelings often seem to go hand in hand. I usually try to combat my boredom by keeping busy – as busy as possible – but that hasn't worked. I just get bored of being busy. Having 101 things to do makes no difference if I find all 101 things boring.

If Carl is right, I need the opposite approach. Instead of trying so hard to be *busy,* working hard to fill up my evenings with social engagements and planning weekends away, I decide to try a period of slowing down, of spending more time at home – even if that means being home alone, and having periods of doing nothing. I watch less TV too (see Idea 8) and instead I simply focus on being. I abandon my "to do" lists and stop putting pressure on myself to make every minute count, to achieve things with my time. I don't really believe it will work. I suspect this will make me feel more bored than ever. But it doesn't. It has the opposite effect. I start to enjoy life more than ever before, as I relax into this change in lifestyle.

Once I stop treating busyness as a virtue, as Olds and Schwartz put it, once I get used to the feeling that I don't need to worry about being quite so productive, I start to notice changes in my life. The biggest change is at mealtimes. I didn't realise how much I enjoyed cooking. It seems that one of the problems of our hectic, modern lives is that it doesn't leave us time to really enjoy our food.

"Instead of sitting down with family or friends," says Carl Honoré, "we often eat solo, on the move or while doing something else – working, driving, reading the newspaper, surfing the net....Americans devote less time than anyone else – about an hour a day – to eating, and are more likely to buy processed food and to dine alone."

As I slow down, cooking ceases to be a chore and becomes a pleasure. Rather than relying on the local Chinese take-away, the freezer and my very obliging housemate to provide my meals, I start to make them from scratch *myself*. We start to eat in the dining room, rather than on the sofa in front of the TV, and we start to enjoy proper conversations over our meals. And I love it. It feels better!

Another advantage of slowing down your lifestyle and not dashing around from one place to the next is that you can use slower modes of transport. "Travelling on foot," according to Carl Honore, "can also be meditative, fostering a slow frame of mind. When we walk, we are aware of the details around us – birds, trees, the sky, shops and houses, other people. We make connections." And that's what finding freedom from loneliness is all about: making connections.

I haven't made any new friends by taking life more slowly, but I feel a stronger sense of connection within my local area because of the people I greet with a simple "Good morning!" when I walk to the Post Office or to the library instead of driving. I'm no longer quite so fearful of boredom, which has always felt to me like loneliness' evil twin. And I'm definitely enjoying my food more!

Idea 22: Increase your self-esteem

Nobody can make you feel inferior without your consent.
~ Eleanor Roosevelt

Feeling lonely seems to go hand in hand with low self-esteem, particularly if the cause of the loneliness is a relationship break-up.

When my husband and I split up, I was left not only feeling lonely, but my self-esteem had taken a real hit too. Suddenly I was full of self doubts: what if I didn't make any new friends? What if no-one ever found me attractive again? What if I was doomed to spend the rest of my life alone? I needed other people to give me love and attention but I simply wasn't getting it so I felt not only lonely, but also unworthy of the love and attention that I craved.

It's another of the catch 22 situations that loneliness seems to cause. My low self-esteem made it harder for me to go out and meet new people. As a result, I felt lonelier than ever before. That seemed to exacerbate my low self-esteem and the whole cycle perpetuated itself.

Losing self-esteem made a difference to the quality of my interactions with other people. Whilst most of my friends stuck by me, I'm sure they were fed up of my neediness. I was always whinging about the same situation – not being able to meet anyone or, if I had met someone, worries that the relationship wasn't going to last. One friend actually told me that I wasn't much fun to be around and I'm sure she was right.

The philosopher Erich Fromm said, "Selfish persons are incapable of loving others, but they are not capable of loving themselves either." Perhaps, I thought, that's it. Perhaps I am still single and all my previous relationships have all failed, because I'm not *capable* of loving anyone else and I'm not capable because I don't love myself enough.

Working through Dr. David Burns' book *Ten Days to Great Self-Esteem* helped me to identify some of the negative ways that I thought about life and about myself. Dr. Burns identifies 10 ways in which our thinking can be distorted such as discounting the positives, jumping to conclusions and "all-or-nothing" thinking. I realised that my thinking fell into the overgeneralisation category: because one relationship had broken up, I assumed that *all* my relationships would be unsuccessful. I labelled myself as someone who failed at relationships and did what Dr. Burns would call "fortune telling" – predicting that *all* my future relationships would end, exactly as this one had. As a result, my self-esteem was rock bottom.

In *The Feeling Good Handbook,* Dr. Burns describes an encounter with a patient suffering from low-self esteem. He had to cancel an appointment with her because a friend of his had died. He called and explained the reason but she was furious and accused him of not caring about her. Whilst it seems totally unreasonable of her to behave like this, I can understand it. She had low self-esteem and his cancellation of the appointment made her feel rejected. I've felt a similar sense of rejection when friends have cancelled social arrangements: their reasons may have been good ones, but I saw the cancellation as a sign that I wasn't important. That wasn't true: it was just my interpretation.

In order to go out into the world, forge new connections with other people and thereby make new friends, I needed to be more resilient to this kind of knock-back. I needed to be able to accept that not everyone I met would want to be my friend and that wasn't a sign that I wasn't worthy of *anyone's* friendship. I needed to accept that my friends would sometimes cancel, due to work, illness or unavoidable family commitments and that wasn't a sign that they didn't care about me. To have that kind of resilience, I needed to improve my self-esteem.

Identifying my negative patterns of thinking and replacing them with more positive thoughts as I worked through the *Ten Days to Great Self-Esteem* book really helped.

The self-help books are full of all sorts of other activities which supposedly improve someone's self-esteem. Most of them haven't worked for me. I haven't found looking at myself naked in the mirror and trying to appreciate my body particularly helpful. Writing affirmations and repeating these positive statements to myself over and over haven't done much for me either.

Some books advocate regularly treating yourself to fresh flowers or a hot bath with bubbles – to show yourself, in the words of the L'Oreal advert, that "you're worth it". I had a long, hot bubble bath after a particularly arduous run recently. My muscles ached less as a result, but it didn't do anything for my self-esteem. Later in this book, I advocate having a hot bath as a cure for loneliness, but there *is* scientific evidence that the feelings of warmth that having a hot bath brings can really ease feelings of loneliness. But I'm not convinced that a hot bath raises levels of self-esteem. They haven't raised mine anyway. I just sit there contemplating my cellulite.

It occurred to me that learning to love myself is perhaps a three step process. Find out who I am. Accept who I am. Love who I am. Earlier I wrote that finding my authentic self was a big part of my finding freedom from loneliness. Self-esteem means, essentially, learning to love yourself. Jesus said, "Love your neighbour as yourself" implying that we *should* also love ourselves. But if I haven't found my authentic self, if I don't know who *I* really am, I *can't* love myself. Once I have found my authentic self – sorry, I know it's a bit of a cliché – I can start to accept myself and maybe then, I will learn to love myself. And perhaps an essential part of learning to love myself is forgiving myself for all the things I *don't* love about myself.

According to Sue Atkinson, author of *Building Self-Esteem:* "We can be so busy 'beating ourselves up' that we are failing to see that, like everybody else, we run best on affirmation and forgiveness. Forgiving ourselves is a hard but necessary process. We need to acknowledge that, like everyone else, we sometimes do get things wrong. As we learn to let those things go, we can accept ourselves as we are. Weak, frail people sometimes, but whatever it is that we might have done for which we feel we need forgiveness, we can get beyond it."

I feel more positive about life and more positive about myself, and, as I feel more positive, I find it easier to make friends. When I talk about being "positive about myself", I don't mean being arrogant. To me, being arrogant means thinking that I'm better than someone else, but being confident and having a healthy sense of self-esteem means really believing that I'm just as good as the next person. Happy, confident people *attract* other people so improving my self-esteem has made it easier to make connections.

Idea 23: Be mindful

By attentive living, we can learn the difference between being present in loneliness and being present in solitude.
~ Henri Nouwen

In September 2011, I found myself bored in Birmingham city centre for a few hours and I ventured into the local branch of Waterstones bookshop. Heading for my favourite section, the one with all the "mind, body, spirit", self-help and religious stuff, I came across a table with the latest books that Waterstones were promoting. It was a table piled high with books on mindfulness.

This struck me as something of a coincidence. A few months before, I'd never even heard of mindfulness, but that day in Birmingham, I was on my way to a mindfulness retreat at the Quaker study centre, Woodbrooke. The retreat was to be led by Buddhist monks from Plum Village, a community in France founded by Thich Nhat Hanh, a Vietnamese monk and author of *The Miracle of Mindfulness*.

Mindfulness, to put it simply, means living in the present moment.

In *The Miracle of Mindfulness*, Thich Nhat Hanh describes watching one of his friends eating a tangerine. At least, I think it was a tangerine, but it could have been any type of citrus fruit. His friend was busy talking at the same time, just shoving each segment of fruit into his mouth and barely noticing as he swallowed it. He didn't savour the taste, the scent or the texture. This is the opposite of mindful eating.

I'm not good at living in the present moment or at savouring what I'm doing at any particular moment. I'm usually thinking about something else. I'm worrying about something that has happened in the past, or I'm worrying about something that might happen in the future.

95

I was in my best mate's van when I'd decided that I simply *had* to go on that mindfulness retreat at Woodbrooke. We were driving off on a shopping trip, planning to visit Ikea and B & Q and Costco. I love going on these trips with him but he is always so busy with his business and his studies that he seldom has time. So this was a rare treat. But I wasn't enjoying it.

I'd met a new man a few weeks before on internet dating and things were not going well. Instead of enjoying the trip, I was pining over my new man. Why hadn't he texted? Why hadn't he phoned? I plagued my best mate with question after question about whether he thought this man really liked me or whether I ought to just end the relationship before I got hurt. I wasn't enjoying the trip at all – I wasn't enjoying the present moment at all. I was going over the past, raking over every conversation I'd had with this new man for signs of whether he really liked me and I was worrying about the future: should I end it? Should I text him? What would happen if I appeared too keen?

I knew that I should be living in the present. If I could just focus my mind on the trip to the shops, I knew I would be happier. But I couldn't. That's when I decided to go on the mindfulness retreat.

Although mindfulness might have its origins in the Buddhist tradition, and although the retreat that I was going on was to be run by Buddhists, it's more than just a religious teaching. Mindfulness is now being used as a therapeutic technique.

On the *Be Mindful* website, Professor Mark Williams from the University of Oxford discusses how mindfulness can be helpful for those suffering from depression. He was initially sceptical, he says, when the subject of mindfulness meditation was first broached but when he actually tried mindfulness meditation himself, he realised how powerful it could be. "For very good theoretical and scientific reasons … it seemed that this particular sort of mental training would get at all the processes that actually were damaging people's mental health. When your mood begins to go down, what happens is all the memories from the past come back as if it was happening now. You just dig yourself deeper into the hole. Mindfulness helps you see the warning signs that you're going there and also teaches you skilful means to dissolve those habits of mind that have bugged you for so long."

As I arrived at the retreat, I wondered what habits of mind I might be able to dissolve. I'd spend the previous night obsessively worrying that my car would get broken into in Birmingham. I have no idea why: Birmingham is no more dangerous than most of the places where I leave my car. But I worried and worried – as I was on the phone to my housemate I was worrying, as I was watching *Strictly Come Dancing* I was worrying and as I was visiting an elderly aunt I was worrying.

Is mind*less* the opposite of mindful? Whatever the word is for the opposite of mindful, that's what I was managing to be. My car *didn't* get broken into and I knew full well that it wasn't because I'd spent all night worrying about it.

I first noticed the effects of living mindfully over breakfast on Day 1 of the retreat. We had to eat mindfully, in silence with no distractions. We were told take our time over our food, chewing slowly and appreciating its sight, smell and taste. It was a buffet breakfast. I have no self-restraint at buffets – I can never stop myself going back for more. I had a large plate of eggs, mushrooms, hash browns and beans, washed down with some orange juice and a large mug of tea. There was a tempting array of pastries on offer and I longed for a croissant, but I knew I was full. Normally, I would have just gone and had a croissant anyway, and been uncomfortably full all morning, but eating slowly had made me much more aware of how my stomach felt. It wasn't just that I *resisted* the croissant. I knew I'd feel better without it.

We learnt walking meditation techniques, we learnt sitting meditation techniques, we learnt mantras. We learnt that it is ok to express your feelings when you're hurt but not if you're still full of anger. We learnt about the Buddha.

97

We learnt about what life is like in the monastery. All very interesting, but nothing, it seemed, to do with loneliness.

Then Brother Ben, who was a bit too good-looking to be a monk and whose rather exotic monk's robes concealed the fact that he was really from Doncaster, asked everyone what spirituality meant for them. People said various things: they mentioned God, they mentioned Buddha, they mentioned meditating, they mentioned there being more to life than just this physical world. Then Brother Ben revealed his answer.

"Spirituality for me," he said, "means a sense of being connected. A feeling that I am not separate from the rest of life."

A sense of being connected. The antidote to loneliness. At the tea break, I pounced on him. I'd never normally pounce quite so eagerly on a man but he was a monk so I felt that my pouncing couldn't be misinterpreted.

"What do you think about loneliness?" I asked, having established that he didn't want to drink his tea mindfully in silence.

He was surprised by the question. I told him about my thoughts – that I wanted to write a book, perhaps even make a documentary and that I'd done lots of research. He said he'd get back to me.

Next day, Brother Ben devoted the whole of the daily "Dharma Talk" to the issue of loneliness. I felt guilty, thinking that the whole room of perhaps 60 or 70 people were all having to sit still for hours and listen to a talk about an issue that was pertinent only to me. But then at the end of the talk, more questions were asked than after any *other* Dharma talk that week. There was a real buzz during the coffee break as people debated what had been said. I clearly *wasn't* the only one who was interested in loneliness.

My usual feeling when loneliness overcomes me is to try and push it away. I'll switch on the computer and see if I've any messages on Facebook. I'll get my phone out – could there be a text or a missed call that I hadn't noticed? I'll put the TV on. I'll push the loneliness away as quickly as I can, trying in vain to get rid of it.

The mindful approach is to *be* with the emotion. To sit with the emotion. Just to be aware that the loneliness is there.

"Be still," advised Brother Ben. "It's like a tree in a storm. Being in the mind is like being in the top of the tree – it's harder to weather the storm up there. Come back down to the trunk. Focus on your breathing. Say to yourself, "I have loneliness" but don't suppress it. Be with that emotion."

I tried it. It helped. Much more than Facebook, my mobile phone and the TV ever did.

I think mindfulness helps in a more general way too. Food tastes better when you eat it slowly and mindfully, preferably without the distraction of TV and even conversation. Music sounds more beautiful when you're really listening to it, rather than just playing it as background whilst you do something else. When you walk in the countryside, and focus only on walking in the countryside, you notice birds singing, trees rustling, the beauty of the world around you.

Instead of focusing on the paucity of connection in my life, when I'm being mindful, I notice how the world around me feels somehow like a much richer place. I didn't really believe that it could work. But it does.

Idea 24: Throw off your conditioning and stop believing the stereotypes

*You have been taught that there is something wrong with you
and that you are imperfect but there isn't and you're not.*
~ Cheri Huber

I'd never even heard of "conditioning" until I came across author Cheri Huber. (She wrote *Be The Person You Want To Find, How To Get From Where You Are To Where You Want To Be* and *There Is Nothing Wrong With You* to name but a few.)

The first one I read was *Be The Person You Want To Find*. To be honest, it was one of a huge pile of books that I bought, hoping to discover how to find Mr Right. I still haven't found Mr Right, but reading Cheri's book, I realised why finding Mr Right was so important to me.

Cheri says her purpose is "to help you see through and be free of your conditioned responses to life" and to find "freedom from all the stuff we learned as children and now drag along with us through life."

How does this relate to my loneliness? A significant part (though not the only part) of my loneliness is my failure to meet and settle down with the right man. I am 42. I thought that I'd be happily married by now and I'm not. I feel like I have missed out on something. Yet I have been actively seeking to find my soulmate since I was a teenager. Perhaps I've wanted to find him a bit too much and that's why he's eluded me.

Where, I wondered reading Cheri's words, did this desperate longing to find my life partner come from? Why do I think my life is less meaningful somehow if I haven't found him? Why has searching for the right man so often been the most important driving force in my life?

My very warm-hearted parents always included a neighbour in our family celebrations and get-togethers. She was a close friend – like family, we'd always say – but I think there was an element of pity in those invitations too.

100

Because she had never married. She had never met the right man. "We won't end up like her," my sister would always say, after one of us had broken up with yet another boyfriend, "we won't, will we?"

I wonder if that's where some of my conditioning comes from. I am not seeking to lay the blame at the door of my parents – far from it. I've come across self-help books that say that people have unhealthy relationships because they had an abusive or alcoholic parent and I think, "Well, that's not me! I had lovely parents!" But somehow the presence of that neighbour, my parents' kindness and the way they so obviously felt sorry for her, gave me the idea as a child that there was nothing worse than ending up as a single woman.

The fact that she was always off travelling the world and going on luxurious cruises and that she didn't have to take anyone else's holiday wishes into account when she did those things – well, that fact just passed me by. The fact that she could enjoy being with my sister and me when we were children but give us back when we got naughty – well, that passed me by too. I didn't see any of the advantages to being single. I just saw being single as a definite no-no. Something that I wanted to avoid.

Perhaps one way of moving from loneliness towards solitude is to acknowledge these rather limiting beliefs and where they have come from. By acknowledging that the culture I grew up in made me believe that marriage was something I should aspire to and staying single well into one's forties was something definitely to be avoided, I can now see why I sometimes feel lonely. I haven't lived up to the expectations I was brought up with: that I *should* get married and live happily ever after. No-one ever taught me that staying single and living happily ever after was a possibility too. Shaking off the belief that you have to be married to be happy allows me to explore the possibility that I might be able to be happy on my own. Loneliness *isn't* an inevitable part of staying on my own.

"How Does Culture Influence the Degree of Romantic Loneliness and Closeness?" asked an article published in The Journal of Psychology in 2008. The writers, Seepersad, Choi and Shin, suggested that "Western cultures promote strong levels of desire for romantic relationships compared with non-Western cultures... Therefore, when a person from a Western culture is not in a romantic relationship, he or she may experience a high level of loneliness because of the intense desire to be in a romantic relationship. Conversely, a person from a non-Western culture may have less of a desire to be in a romantic relationship and thus less feelings of loneliness."

So perhaps growing up in a Western culture also accounts for the fact that I have, for the whole of my adult life, placed *so* much emphasis on finding a romantic relationship. The culture surrounding me, from the chick-lit novels I've read to the romantic comedies that I've watched in the cinema, have encouraged me to focus on this aspect of my life. The fact that my expectations haven't been met might not seem so important if the culture around me hadn't *made* it seem so important.

"In Western culture, in which romantic relationships are heavily emphasized," the article continues, "lonely individuals often assume that the reason for their loneliness is the lack of a romantic partner. The results of the present study suggest that it is not only the absence of a romantic partner that causes such strong feelings of loneliness but also the social expectation of having a romantic partner."

Perhaps if I changed my expectations, if I could somehow let go of the idea that I *need* a romantic partner to be happy in life, perhaps then my loneliness would cease to be such a problem.

I wonder if we're also socially conditioned to see being alone in general as a problem. The child who doesn't socialise easily and who stands alone in the playground at playtimes is a source of much discussion and concern on parents' evenings. No-one ever stops to ask if that child just *prefers* being alone sometimes.

In *Positive Solitude*, Rae Andre suggests that, "...as the parent tries to encourage the child to be independent, the parent may unthinkingly say something like, 'You're not afraid to be alone are you?' or 'Are you sure you'll be all right alone?' Of this question the child may think, 'Am I old enough to be alone or not? Is there something to be frightened of when I am alone?'"

As I grew up, I actually remember my parents saying this sort of thing to me. I'm sure they did so with the most loving intentions. I look back on my school days and remember the days when my best friend Sharon was off sick. I wasn't the sort of child who made friends easily so if Sharon wasn't there, I'd have no-one else to play with and would spend the playtimes alone. When I came home, my dad would make a big deal of this, trying to cheer me up because he felt sorry for me. He didn't mean any harm by this – the opposite in fact. He was trying to comfort me. But nevertheless, this experience told me that being alone was bad. If you were alone, you were someone to be pitied.

Sometimes my parents would go off on a shopping trip and I'd be quite content to stay at home and watch ballet videos. And my parents *would* ask, as Rae Andre suggests, if I was going to be ok on my own. Did I perhaps subconsciously get the message that I *shouldn't* feel quite so content to stay home alone? Perhaps I felt that I ought to like going to discos, that I ought to be going out with boys and that I ought to have a big group of friends to socialise with. But really, I enjoyed making things, doing my flute practice and having friendships on more of a one-on-one basis.

Realising where my beliefs about aloneness come from has made my loneliness easier to deal with. I've stopped trying to be someone who enjoys discos and wants to hang out with a big group of mates and focused on being who I really am: someone who likes to meet up with a close friend and have deep, intimate conversations, but who also *likes* spending time alone. It's taking longer to shake off the belief that I have to find my soulmate in order for my life to be meaningful but at least I know where I've got this idea from.

There's such a stereotype attached to loneliness and I grew up with that stereotype: that a child playing on their own was slightly odd and that a single woman was an unhappy woman – lonely, needy, desperate, full of regrets about never having met the right man, self-centred, lazy, lacking in get up and go, unable to make friends and generally not nice to be around. Some of the self-help literature about loneliness actually reinforces those beliefs. I long to have a ceremonial bonfire of all self-help books that suggest, usually in the most patronising tone possible, that learning to make friends is the way out of the loneliness trap and that those of us who feel lonely are simply lacking in social skills.

I *have* friends, good friends too. Yet I still feel lonely sometimes. It *is* true that social skills haven't come easily to me (some ideas about that later) but if it were *that* simple, we'd all just learn good social skills and no-one would be lonely.

In Emily White's book *Lonely: A Memoir* she cites various studies that show that lonely people are no less attractive, smart or popular than non-lonely people. Yet too often we believe that the lonely person is odd in some way: not good at making friends, ridiculously shy, socially inept. When I'm feeling lonely, I sometimes fall into the trap of believing that there *is* something wrong with me.

"Historically, people have lived with other people as it's safer, easier to find food and shelter," writes Rae Andre. "But today, people can feed, clothe and house themselves on their own perfectly well. More and more households are single households. However, our psychology has not caught up with this: few of us have the psychological tools to live happily alone. Society continues to give us the message that we are 'on the wrong path'. "

PART 3:
MAKE CONNECTIONS
WITH OTHER
PEOPLE

Idea 25: Have a good laugh a day

Laughter is not primarily about humour, but about social relationships.
~ Robert Provine, neuroscientist

Having a good laugh at least once a day is yet another of the tips from the "Happiness Manifesto" in the TV programme *Making Slough Happy*. It's also recommended by Rae Andre in her book, *Positive Solitude: A Practical Program for Mastering Loneliness and Achieving Self-Fulfilment*

But Andre admits that, "For people alone, finding opportunities to experience joy and laughter is more challenging."

Personally, I initially found the idea that I could help ease my loneliness simply by watching a sitcom or looking at a few cartoons rather preposterous. However, there have been scientific studies proving that laughter has a positive effect on both our levels of happiness *and* our physical health.

Researchers at Oxford University, led by evolutionary psychologist Robin Dunbar, discovered that the ability to belly laugh was probably unique to early humans. They believe that this allowed our ancestors to form much larger tribal groupings than the ape-like species that lived alongside them. Could it be that laughter helps us to form connections with other human beings? Social laughter, Robin Dunbar suggests, is "grooming at a distance." It helps us to form and maintain bonds with each other.

Whilst loneliness has been shown to have a negative effect on our physical health, laughter seems to have a corresponding positive effect. Two of the physical effects that loneliness causes are an increase in the stress hormone cortisol and consequently, a weaker immune system. Laughter, on the other hand, has been shown to reduce cortisol levels and boost the number of antibody-producing cells, thereby strengthening the immune system. In other words, laughter seems to cause physical effects that are the *opposite* of the physical effects that loneliness causes.

According to Robin Dunbar, it's not the intellectual pleasure of humour that produces such positive effects on our health, but the physical act of laughing itself. The simple muscular exertions involved in laughter trigger an increase in endorphins, the brain chemicals famous for their feel-good effect. Chocolate, incidentally, is also said to increase the production of endorphins so when I can't find anything to laugh at, it's a good excuse to tuck into a bar of Galaxy.

And sometimes, I just *can't* find anything to laugh at. Sitcoms, with the exception of *Father Ted,* don't really do it for me: some of them, quite frankly, don't even make me so much as smile. I find myself wondering if I've got a sense of humour at all - in fact, I feel like the character Margot in the TV series *The Good Life,* constantly whinging, "I just don't get it!"

Apparently the key is to fake it. Studies show that the positive effects of smiling happen whether the smile is fake or real, and the same goes for laughter.

I'm not sure how I feel about being home alone, sitting on my sofa and pretending to laugh. Perhaps next time I'm feeling a bit down, if it isn't time for *The News Quiz* on Radio 4, I'll give the fake laughter a try and see if it really does reduce my feelings of loneliness.

Idea 26: Find a community

What should young people do with their lives today? ... the most daring thing is to create stable communities in which the terrible disease of loneliness can be cured."
~ Kurt Vonnegut

The place where I live has a big, big impact on my level of loneliness. Living within easy reach of my family members (though I don't have that many) and close friends is obviously going to make seeing them easier so I'm going to feel less lonely. But I don't think that's the only way in which my geographical position can help me.

There are some areas in the country where people smile and say good morning to strangers they pass on the street. The area where I live is quite good for that but the North-East is even better. Whenever I go to the North-East, I can't get over how friendly people are. But there are other areas – I'm thinking big city centres in particular - where people seem to go to great lengths to avoid even making eye contact. There's an episode in Christopher Jamison's book, *Finding Happiness* where a teenage girl with Down's syndrome is on a London tube train with her family. She is smiling and laughing and asking people on the tube if they feel happy. Virtually no-one meets her gaze or answers her question. No-one smiles back.

Big cities, where people do not make eye contact, smile or say "Good morning" to passing strangers, make all of us feel lonely to a certain extent. Of course, I'm not saying that living in the capital is the only cause of loneliness or that living in a small Northern village where the neighbours all greet each other by name will cure loneliness, but I do think that where you live makes a difference to how you feel.

According to Robert E. Lane of Yale University, it isn't certain whether "the anonymity of big cities is worse than the isolation of farm areas" but "loneliness seems to be least often experienced in suburbs of big cities, rather than in villages beloved of small communities advocates."

I've never lived in the centre of a big city or on an isolated farm, but I have lived in a village and in the suburbs of both London and Manchester, and my experience bears out what Robert Lane says. I was much lonelier in the village than I was in either of the suburbs. In the village, even after three years of living there, I still felt like an outsider. In the suburbs, I settled down really quickly and enjoyed being near the hustle and bustle of the city centre, but returning to the smaller community of the suburb afterwards. I love the myriad of activities that cities, especially London, have to offer, but I like going home to a place where my neighbours greet me as I park the car and ask how my day went.

If I go running in my local park, it is unusual for me to return having spoken to no-one. Almost always, a passing dog-walker will give me a friendly word of encouragement. "Keep it up, love," they'll shout. "You're doing great!" A trip to the Post Office inevitably involves a chat to someone else in the queue. It might be a superficial conversation. It has never yet been the start of a deep and meaningful friendship, but it's something. Face to face interaction in a world that seems to run on call centres and filling in forms on the internet.

We all dream – well, I do anyway – of having a local bar that's like "Cheers" in the old American sitcom of the same name. As the theme song says, "You want to go where everybody knows your name." Sadly, I don't have a local pub like that, where I can walk in confidently, be greeted by some friendly faces, and say to the landlord, "The usual please!" But I was surprised and delighted when I walked into my local library one day, and the librarian said, "Oh a book's come for you!" before I had produced my ticket with my name on it. She already *knew* my name.

I have no local friends other than my housemate. I don't know anyone in my town whose door I could just go and knock on if I fancied a cup of tea. Yet I feel "socially embedded" as I think psychologists and social scientists call it, just because of those chats in the Post Office, the librarian who knew my name and the encouraging dog-walkers.

I know my housemate will want to move on from here before too long, and, since it's his house, I'll have to find a new place and probably I'll have to face up to living on my own again. I'm not sure I'm looking forward to that. Let's face it: sometimes it's lonely.

But I'm hoping that thinking about why I find it difficult and what factors increase my feelings of loneliness will allow me to make an informed decision about where I want to live.

I need an area with things going on, things to do almost every night of the week: art classes, salsa lessons, reading groups, language classes, meetings or lectures. I might not necessarily do all of those things, but they're a safety net, something to fall back on. I need to know that I don't have to be alone within my own four walls. Good outside spaces are important to me too: parks to run in and beautiful scenery to walk in. I'd like a river or a lake nearby because I find water calming. I need a public transport system with easy and frequent access so that I can go out and have a glass of wine and not worry about driving home. I'd like somewhere that feels safe so that I'm not afraid as I unlock my front door after a night out.

The places available to shop in make a huge difference too. Just the act of buying vegetables at a farm shop or some cheese at a local market can provide an opportunity for a friendly conversation. How much nicer than an impersonal supermarket! A few craft shops can be a source of inspiration on an afternoon when I'm feeling bored. Is it just a coincidence that statistics show that our society is getting lonelier at the same time as more and more of our town centres are taken over by chain stores and the giant supermarkets force the friendly, local shopkeepers out of business?

There *are* places in the UK where inspirational things are going on, inspirational things that seem to foster a real sense of community. I'm thinking of the Incredible

Edible project of Todmorden, in West Yorkshire, where everyone is encouraged to get involved with community gardening and the whole town is dotted with vegetable gardens where you can help yourself to produce. Or the Chorlton Good Neighbours scheme which has been running for over 40 years in the South Manchester suburb and aims to offer friendship and support to anyone who needs it. Chorlton, Todmorden and nearby Hebden Bridge are all on my list as potential places to move to and that's partly because of those kinds of initiatives.

A friend of mine always jokes that her ideal would be to live in a commune. Not the stereotypical hippy-style commune, but perhaps to have a flat in a small building where her friends live in all the other flats of the building. When I watch too many episodes of *Grand Designs* and *Homes under the Hammer,* and find myself browsing the catalogues of the local auction houses, I sometimes see grand, old properties for sale which would be great to convert into flats. I fantasise sometimes about whether I could make my friend's dream a reality. Wouldn't it be amazing to gather a group of friends together and enjoy community living in a way that also allowed you to have your own space?

As with all my good ideas, someone has got there first. There are co-housing projects springing up all over the country. The Lilac project in Leeds, for instance, aims to build low impact housing *and* foster a sense of community living and the Older Woman's Co-Housing Project is creating a co-housing community in High Barnet to promote living both co-operatively *and* independently.

My gut instinct that where I live makes a difference to how I feel is borne out by scientific research. "Changing UK" is a report compiled by a team led by Professor Danny Dorling at the University of Sheffield on behalf of the BBC. The report considered how communities have changed over 40 years and how feelings of isolation are increasing in different areas of Britain. It measured "anomie" – an academic term for estimating the percentage of people who feel a poor sense of belonging to an area. The researchers

111

created "loneliness indices" and top of the league was Edinburgh with a score of 33.1%. In contrast, Bramhall, a commuter suburb near Manchester, scored only 14.96%. It is incidentally very close to the suburb where I lived very happily on my own in the first few years after my divorce.

One of my friends grew up in Bramhall and her parents still live there. She was very surprised when I told her that statistic but then when I asked her if she'd ever been lonely, she admitted that she hadn't. Perhaps there's something in those stats. Of course, we can't all move to Bramhall, but I do think that these are the sorts of factors I need to consider when I'm planning my next move because they have such a big impact on my levels of happiness and on my levels of loneliness.

I'm not saying "Move house and you won't be lonely ever again." For one thing, moving isn't always practical. People have ties like work, children settled in a school, elderly relatives who need caring for and negative equity. And of course moving itself can be a cause of great stress and often loneliness. You might find an area that would suit you better but it's a long way away from your closest friend who is currently only 2 streets away. As Robert E. Lane put it: "Those who move are more lonely than those who remain in the same neighbourhood for a long time."

But when I next need to move house, keeping my loneliness at bay must play a big part in determining where I should live. I'm not going to let house prices, proximity to work and the glossy photos on Rightmove.co.uk be the only factors when deciding the property I choose. Finding a house in an area with that all important feeling of community is far more important to me than off-street parking and an en-suite.

Idea 27: Join something

*Do not join encounter groups. If you enjoy being made to feel
inadequate, call your mother.*
~ Liz Smith

Almost all the books I read on loneliness suggested learning
new techniques for making new friends, learning to enjoy
being on your own and joining a club. All good ideas and all
included in this book.

The thing is, I didn't think I had a problem making
new friends and I simply didn't enjoy being on my own and
as for joining a club – well, I just couldn't find the energy or
the courage to go out and join something sociable like a
club. Joining a club would take motivation and I was
completely out of motivation. I knew it might help, but
finding the get up and go to do anything felt about as
impossible as motivating myself to climb up Snowdon when
I could just as easily take that little train that goes up to the
summit.

There was no guarantee that joining a group would
make me feel less lonely, anymore than there was a
guarantee that I would get a clear view if I *did* reach the top
of Snowdon. Actually, I suspected that joining a group
might make me feel a whole lot worse. At least initially. And
as it happens, when I did eventually join a group, it *did* make
me feel worse in the beginning.

It wasn't easy to find a group. Although I found
masses of groups that I *could* have joined – the Meetup
website and Facebook were full of them – it took a while to
find a group that really appealed to me. I tried starting my
own group, which, according to psychiatrists, Jacqueline
Olds and Richard Schwartz is "a particularly effective route
to alleviating loneliness and isolation for those who know
people with whom they would like to socialise but seldom
see because of the demands of family, work and otherwise
frantic and incompatible schedules." I met an elderly

113

Catholic lady who had been divorced for several decades. Life got lonely sometimes, she admitted, but one way she'd found to overcome this was to initiate monthly Sunday lunches for other single and divorced friends. But my efforts to organise monthly girls' night outs for myself and a group of ex-colleagues didn't last beyond the first two months.

So I plucked up courage and I joined an existing group. It was a general, social group, aimed at injecting a bit more fun and activity into people's lives. Most people, but not all, were single. The trouble was, at the first meeting, everyone knew each other and I didn't know anyone. Friendships were already established, social ties were strong and gossip was being exchanged. I couldn't participate in conversations because I didn't know the other people being talked about. I'm not saying it was unwelcoming – it wasn't. It was the sort of group I *wanted* to be a part of – the members clearly *had* forged meaningful connections with each other. But as a new person, it was difficult to infiltrate.

I had three choices. Give up on the group thing altogether, try another group where social ties were not so strong and where it was easier to fit in as a new member or persist with the original group in the hope that I would become part of things and start to make friends. Trying another group where social ties weren't so strong seemed pointless. I might feel less of an outsider at the initial few meetings, but I reckoned I would be unlikely to make real connections there. I didn't want to quit straight away so I chose the last option – I went back to the original group.

For the first few weeks, I felt like an outsider and had a stronger sense of loneliness than ever before. I struggled to remember the names of people I met, but they struggled to remember mine too so it didn't seem to matter – well, except to me. I got a bit tired of reminding people who I was. People would start conversations in front of me, talking across me and discussing someone they both knew and I didn't. In-jokes would be made that I didn't get. They'd talk about other events that they'd been on that I

114

hadn't or refer to a shared confidence. They weren't deliberately excluding me, but I felt excluded.

No matter how welcoming the group is, how open the members are to letting new people in and no matter how charming I was or how well developed my social skills, I couldn't instantly expect to fit in, I realised. So I felt lonely. Lonelier in the group than if I'd stayed at home and spent the evening on the sofa watching Coronation Street with a bottle of wine and a large bag of Kettle Chips.

But there came a point when going out to meet up with the group *did* feel more inviting than a bag of Kettlechips – even than a bag of sea salt with crushed black peppercorns Kettlechips. Suddenly, people *did* know my name and I was included in conversations.

Finding the right group is a bit of a catch 22. If the group is the sort of group where people make real friendships, when you first go, you feel like a bit of an outsider. Yet that's the type of group you need to find because that's the type of group where *you'll* make real friendships. And I did. I left the group eventually as I'd lost interest in the types of activities that they did. But I stayed friends – good friends too – with two of the people I met there. Ultimately it was worth joining just to meet those two people.

But I wouldn't have met those two people if I'd not persevered beyond the initial phase of feeling like the new girl. I didn't realise this until recently. I look back at the various things I've tried in the name of meeting new people - salsa lessons, the tennis club, various churches, running club, charity fundraising committees – and I realise that I left all of them too soon. When I didn't instantly feel part of things, I dismissed the group as "too clicky" or "not for me".

Of course, a group *might* be too clicky. It might be that I will never fit in with a particular group of people no matter how hard I try, and that continuing to try would be like trying to get the proverbial round peg into the proverbial square hole. But given a bit of effort, sticking with something beyond the first awkward few meetings,

115

might actually lead to me feeling like I am a part of it, that I belong.

Or I might get something else from it. I might never feel like I'm really part of the in-crowd at salsa, but I might get really good at the steps! Perhaps that's why psychiatrists Jacqueline Olds and Richard Schwartz counsel against joining a group *simply* to meet new people and advise finding one in which you have a genuine interest: "If your goal is to meet other single men and women, joining a singles group may seem the obvious answer but there are other routes that can be equally successful. You might opt instead for a group that devotes itself to a cause in which you believe. In the singles group you are sure to meet other single people. But in the bird-watching group, the amateur theatre company, the neighbourhood improvement group, or the political action committee, you will meet people who share your concerns and interests and are willing to explore them together. Some of them may just turn out to be single, but even if they aren't, you have begun the work of creating a social network."

So from now on, I'll be persevering for longer with any group I do join but I won't be joining anything if my *only* motivation is to meet new people. It is far more effective to join something where I'm actually interested in the activity itself, so that making new friends is the bi-product rather than the goal. Salsa classes and writing workshops are therefore in, but you won't catch me near a tennis court or a climbing wall ever again.

Idea 28: Use technology wisely

*Technology is seductive when what it offers meets
our human vulnerabilities.*
~ Sherry Turkle, *Alone Together*

Some days, I love technology. I love the internet. I've no-one at home to talk to so I log onto a social networking site like Facebook, a forum connected with something I'm interested it in or even internet dating, and I get talking to other people out there. The internet helps me to make connections. I'm far from home on a work trip and I get lots of texts from my friends and I don't feel lonely in my hotel room anymore. I'm away on holiday, backpacking in Africa on my own, and those emails from home really keep me going.

The findings on technology and its impact on loneliness are a bit contradictory to say the least. Some people say that the internet really helps their loneliness: if someone is disabled and not able to leave the house, for example, talking to other people online who are in a similar position might be a fantastic opportunity to make friends. There are Meetup groups, internet forums, chat-rooms … a whole host of ways to connect with others. The internet *can* be a fantastic way of finding people to meet up with in the real world, on a face-to-face basis (and taking appropriate measures to protect your personal safety of course.)

"The internet works best when it's used to extend other ways of connecting rather than replace them," point out Jacqueline Olds and Richard Schwartz in their book *The Lonely American.*

The internet allows us to create networks of people who are not tied down to one particular place. However unusual your hobby, you can find a network of people online who share it. But this in turn reduces both the likelihood and need for face-to-face visits with friends and family. A conversation on Skype is not the same as a

117

conversation over a beer in the pub. It might be a great way to talk to your loved ones if they're on the other side of the globe, but it doesn't replace the connection you feel when you're talking to someone who is in the same room as you.

What's more, communicating by text or email isn't always the *best* way to communicate. I learnt this recently when I phoned my mother. To my surprise, when she heard it was me, her tone became a little frosty. I asked what the problem was. "That text," she told me. "It really upset me." I had no recollection of having sent any text that might have upset her. I apologized, and when the conversation ended, I scrolled through my sent messages. The text in question had been intended as a joke. I was teasing her about something my father had said, but I'd hoped she'd have realized this from the multiple exclamation marks I'd used. If I'd made the same remark in person or on the phone, the misunderstanding – and the upset – would have been avoided. She'd have known from my tone of voice that I was being silly.

"The advantage of a phone call or a drop-by over e-mail is clearly greatest when there is trouble at hand," wrote science journalist Daniel Goleman in the *New York Times* in 2007. "But there are ways in which e-mail may subtly encourage such trouble in the first place. This is becoming more apparent with the emergence of social neuroscience, the study of what happens in the brains of people as they interact. New findings have uncovered a design flaw at the interface where the brain encounters a computer screen: there are no online channels for the multiple signals the brain uses to calibrate emotions. Face-to-face interaction, by contrast, is information-rich. We interpret what people say to us not only from their tone and facial expressions, but also from their body language and pacing, as well as their synchronization with what we do and say. In contrast to a phone call or talking in person, e-mail can be emotionally impoverished when it comes to nonverbal messages that add nuance and valence to our words."

It's easy to make connections online. It's quick and convenient to communicate. But those communications are usually not as powerful as real face-to-face interactions. "We enjoy continual connection but rarely have each other's full attention," says author and clinical psychologist Sherry Turkle in her book *Alone Together*. "We have many new encounters but may come to experience them as tentative, to be put 'on hold' if better ones come along...We brag about how many we have 'friended' on Facebook, yet Americans say they have fewer friends than before....The ties we form through the Internet are not, in the end, the ties that bind. But they are the ties that preoccupy."

Connections that are made online are easily severed. If someone annoys you on Facebook, it's very easy to "unfriend" them, cutting them out of your social network. "Digital connections," says Sherry Turkle, "offer the illusion of companionship without the demands of friendship."

We've evolved to feel safer in numbers and to like being in the company of other human beings. Communicating via email or text message does not seem to provide us with the same quality of connection as actually being with someone. Or as Emily White puts it in *Lonely: A Memoir*: "As humans we're hardwired to seek out a sense of togetherness and community, and it's unlikely that internet communications can fulfil that need. If you're staring down a lion, you need someone nearby with a tranquilizer gun, not someone sending encouragements on their Blackberry."

Sometimes I think I place too much emphasis on my virtual connections at the expense of my real ones. I mean, when I'm on the phone to someone, I sometimes sneakily send an email to someone else. Or when my housemate comes in to my room for a chat, I find my attention wandering onto the screen of my laptop, reading the latest updates on Facebook. It seems ridiculous that I would allow a virtual connection to take precedence over a real one.

I'm not the only one who does this. I get really irritated when, sitting in a bar in the middle of a deep and

119

meaningful conversation, my friend's phone beeps and she breaks off our conversation to check her texts. Why? Is it likely to be something that cannot wait? Since when has communicating through technology meant more to us than face-to-face interaction?

In *Alone Together*, Sherry Turkle describes how she was approached by a student at a psychology conference who wanted to know about the current state of research on robots that were designed as human companions.

> She confirmed that she would trade her boyfriend 'for a sophisticated Japanese robot' if the robot would produce what she called 'caring behaviour'. She did not want to be alone. She said, 'If the robot could provide the environment, I would be happy to help produce the illusion that there is somebody really with me.' She was looking for a 'no-risk relationship' that would stave off loneliness.

Perhaps online interactions do provide no-risk relationships for those who do not want to risk the real thing – but isn't it more fulfilling to risk the real thing?

There are times when using technology has helped me with my loneliness. During the 2000 petrol strike, I had just moved to a village in the countryside, I knew no-one, there was no petrol in the car and I couldn't get any more. I was very lonely, and technology felt like a godsend. It was literally the only way I could communicate with friends and family, the only way of getting that sense of connection. I suppose for someone isolated because of illness, disability or simply geography, technology might fulfil a similar function. I've discovered an excellent forum recently on the *Web of Loneliness* website.

At other times, I've used the internet to help me make face-to-face connections. I've found social groups through surfing the net. Once or twice I've made contact with someone through Facebook – a friend of a friend perhaps – got chatting online and then decided to meet in real life. And I can't count the number of dates I've had as a result of doing internet dating.

However, when I've chosen to stay home and surf the net, *instead* of going out and making face-to-face connections with other people in the real world, I've felt lonelier. Staying home and going online is sometimes a more appealing option, especially on a cold winter's night. And it's just plain easier too. Walking into a room of twenty people on my own to do a salsa class is daunting so I stay home and log onto Hotmail and hope some of my friends are online.

But if I find that no-one is online, if I've got no messages, then the technology makes me feel worse. It can be pretty demoralising, day after day, to log onto an internet dating site and find that no-one has messaged you. You haven't got so much as an online wink. I was pretty fed up when I first joined Facebook and could only find 3 people I knew, but each of those people knew over 200 other people. Some people have *thousands* of friends. Sometimes, I look at other people's Facebook walls and they are inundated with countless chirpy messages from *their* friends whilst not one person has even bothered to message me. I recently asked in my status: "Am I invisible?" Admittedly, I did get messages then. But technology does make me pretty miserable if a few days go by and no-one has sent me an email or a text message to see how I'm doing. That's an example of how technology can really exacerbate my loneliness.

Perhaps it's because we now live in a world of communications where everyone is available 24/7 that I now *expect* everyone to contact me 24/7. My self- esteem takes a real nose-dive if I don't get any texts.

The trouble with feeling lonely is that it makes me feel really sensitive about all this kind of stuff. If I didn't feel lonely, I might not notice if my phone doesn't ring for a day or two. I might not look at everyone else's status updates on Facebook and think that everyone else seems to be having a really fantastic social life so why aren't I?

121

I was struck by some words of the 19th century writer, Henry David Thoreau:

> When our life ceases to be inward and private, conversation degenerates into mere gossip…In proportion as our inward life fails, we go more constantly and desperately to the post office. You may depend on it, that the poor fellow who walks away with the greatest number of letters proud of his extensive correspondence has not heard from himself this long while.

Perhaps my addiction to texts and emails are the 21st century equivalent of Thoreau's neighbour walking away with the huge pile of letters from the post office. Perhaps I am constantly looking for connection with other people through technology, because I am not always in touch with my inner self. Perhaps I need to use technology to help me find connections, rather than looking to it to fulfil my need for constant communication, reassurance and validation from other people. I need to remember that the internet and its social networking sites are not yardsticks against which to measure my social acceptability and on which to base my self-esteem; rather they are fantastically useful tools that can help me connect.

Idea 29: Have real conversations

Ultimately the bond of all companionship,
whether in marriage or in friendship, is conversation.
~ Oscar Wilde

In *Making Slough Happy*, one of the top tips in the "Happiness Manifesto" was: "Take time to talk - have an hour-long conversation with a loved one each week."

"Every minute you chat with someone," says evolutionary psychologist Professor Robin Dunbar, "you are saying to them: 'I like being with you, I want you in my social network'. It's the human equivalent of chimpanzees grooming each other to check for fleas."

I'm not exactly known for being quiet, so I've always thought that there was enough talking in my life. For a start, I live with my best friend, and although he's not my partner, we see each other every day. Because I live with him, I've always assumed that I talked to him more than enough (I'm sure *he* thinks it's more than enough!) But I realised recently that I never actually make time to talk to him, in the way I make social arrangements with my other friends. Sometimes our conversations consist simply of "Good morning! Did you sleep well?" I might enquire what he's doing that day – where he's working and whether he'll be home for dinner. He might ask if I'm going out that night.

According to Matthias Mehl, a psychologist at the University of Arizona, the *quality* of our conversations really matter: people who spend more of their day having deep discussions seem to be happier than people who spend their time engaging in small talk.

This is perhaps counterintuitive. You might have expected that people who are thinking and talking about the bigger questions of life and delving into the existential depths might be less happy than those who are talking about shallower, more trivial things like what they'll have for tea, the weather and what was on TV last night.

Dr. Mehl's idea that less small talk leads to greater happiness was based on a study of 79 college students. The group, a mixture of men and women, wore an electronically activated device with a microphone on their lapel that recorded 30-second snippets of conversation every 12.5 minutes for four days, creating what Dr. Mehl called "an acoustic diary of their day." The participants' levels of well-being were also assessed by Dr. Mehl's team.

About 23,000 recordings were acquired over 4 days. The conversations were then classified as either small talk (e.g. conversations about the weather or a TV programme) or more substantive (e.g. conversations about current affairs, philosophy, religion or education). Some conversations were purely practical, such as questions about homework, and at other times, there seemed to be some crossover e.g. a conversation about a TV programme might be considered substantive if it included analysis of the characters and their motivations.

Dr. Mehl discovered that almost half of the conversations that the happiest person in his study had were deep and meaningful. Small talk made up only 10 per cent of their conversations. In comparison, small talk made up over a quarter of the unhappiest person's conversations and more substantive conversations only about a fifth. The results were published in the journal *Psychological Science*.

Dr. Mehl proposes that deep and meaningful conversations might hold the key to happiness for two main reasons. Firstly, as human beings, we are driven to find and create meaning in our lives. Secondly, we are social animals - we need to connect with other people. The study was only small, so it doesn't prove that there is a cause-and-effect relationship between someone's level of happiness and the depth of their conversation. We don't know if people can actually make themselves happier by having more deep and meaningful conversations. It could be that if you're happy to start with, you're more likely to engage in these types of conversations. But if deeper conversations can help us to feel more connected to other people, they might help us find freedom from loneliness.

"By engaging in meaningful conversations, we manage to impose meaning on an otherwise pretty chaotic world," says Dr. Mehl. "And interpersonally, as you find this meaning, you bond with your interactive partner, and we know that interpersonal connection and integration is a core fundamental foundation of happiness."

Neuro-scientists have a possible explanation as to why conversations are so crucial to our levels of happiness, according to Daniel Menaker, author of *A Good Talk*. Oxytocin, otherwise known as the "trust hormone", the "love hormone" and the "cuddle hormone", is secreted during orgasms and breast-feeding. Since I don't have a child, and these days the opportunities to have an orgasm with another human being are few and far between, this seems somewhat irrelevant to me, but says Menaker, there is hope for me yet:

> ...the intense bonding involved in breast-feeing and sex do actually bear indirectly, but closely, on oxytocin's relevance to conversation. For just as those two primal functions ... raise the level, so does – voilà– conversation. I mean, if you sit down with someone and have a good talk, your sense of well-being afterward has not only a conscious component, but a neuro-chemical one as well.

It's not always easy in everyday life to find the time and the opportunity to have anything more than a quick chat with people. I've tried in various train stations and doctors' waiting rooms to initiate a "deep and meaningful conversation" with a complete stranger and got myself some pretty odd looks. But guests at the "conversation dinners" of Theodore Zeldin get to do just that.

Professor Zeldin, a historian and philosopher, believes that changing the way people talk to each other can make the world a better place. There are, he believes, substantial social benefits from getting away from small talk and into the types of substantive conversations that Dr. Mehl was measuring in his study. Zeldin wants people to talk about who they really are and what they want from life and he calls this 'new conversation.'

Zeldin is president of the Oxford Muse, which organizes 'conversation dinners'. At these dinners, you are seated next to someone whom you've never met. It's like the opposite of speed-dating. Instead of rushing from person to person with only a few minutes with each, you spend several hours talking to the person next to you. The other difference with speed-dating is that the aim isn't to fall in love with anyone by the end of the evening.

You are each given a Menu of Conversation: instead of descriptions of food dishes, there are 25 suggested topics of conversation. For example, you might find yourself discussing "When have you felt isolated and what do you do about it?" or "What would make the world a better place and how could you make that happen?"

Zeldin believes that the "new conversation" will break down isolation and alienation and help build a sense of community – surely a step towards a less lonely society in which we can all feel better connected?

Idea 30: Improve your social skills

The power of listening is the power to change hearts and minds. More consequentially, it is the power of giving people what they most desire – to be heard and understood.
~ How to Win Friends and Influence People
in the Digital Age

I've read conflicting reports when it comes to the relationship between loneliness and social skills. Some studies come to the conclusion that lonely people have poorer social skills than those people who aren't lonely. Others have found that there's no correlation between poor social skills and loneliness i.e. the social skills of lonely people are no different from those of non-lonely people. Poor social skills might be *one* possible cause of loneliness, but they aren't the *only* cause of loneliness as you might be led to believe if you read some self-help literature on the topic.

I have to admit that my social skills haven't always been great. I was accused of having no empathy by one friend a few years ago and I haven't seen her since, despite efforts to rekindle the friendship on my part. Looking back on my life, I have stayed in touch with only one friend from my school days (though another has recently contacted me on Facebook) and I haven't kept in touch with anyone at all from university. When you consider that studying at university took up a whole 7 years of my life - I didn't set out to do that long or I might as well have been an architect or a doctor - that's a pretty poor track record.

It might seem as I write about my friendships that I have loads and loads of friends. I do *now*. But in fact, with the exception of only four people - the school friend mentioned above, the woman who was my baby-sitter when I was little, another friend who I met in my late twenties and a former colleague whom I became close to in my early

127

thirties – *all* of my friendships have developed in the last seven years, i.e. since my divorce.

According to Louise C. Hawkley and John T. Cacioppo from the University of Chicago, one theory is that "…loneliness arises from social skill deficits and personality traits that impair the formation and maintenance of social relationships. Social skills research has shown that loneliness is associated with more self-focus, poorer partner attention skills, a lack of self-disclosure to friends, especially among females, and less participation in organized groups, especially among males."

I suspect that it was *my* poor social skills that led to the paucity of friendships in the first three and a half decades of my life.

The subject of social skills presents us with yet another of the catch 22 situations that seem to come with loneliness: the more you need to make connections with others, the harder it becomes to make those connections. Poor social skills are not only a potential cause of loneliness but they're a potential *result* of loneliness as well. Perhaps that's why it's been so difficult for scientists to come up with a definitive answer to the question: is loneliness caused by a lack of social skills? Or could it be that loneliness weakens our social skills? It's a chicken and egg kind of question really.

My loneliness might have been caused, at least initially, by having poor social skills, but my poor social skills are made even worse by my loneliness. It's a vicious circle. Feeling lonely makes me feel anxious to make connections at social events. That anxiety makes me feel shy or it makes me come across as too keen or a bit needy. I become more nervous around people and that makes socialising hard. These days, for example, I find it really difficult to use the telephone and I seldom answer my mobile as a result. So when friends ring to invite me out, I often miss out on the invitations.

That friend telling me I lacked empathy was a wake-up call. I know that's just the way I'm made – some people just don't have much empathy, those with autistic

128

spectrum disorders for example. But, when my friend said that and then disappeared out of my life, I made a conscious effort to do something about my social skills, especially my inability to empathise. I was fed up of not feeling like I fitted in. I was fed up of being wary in my friendships, feeling that I might inadvertently offend someone and then lose them from my life. It was time to do something about it.

1. Be a good listener

If I could see a videotape of myself as a child interacting with other children, I suspect that I'd see that I did all the talking.

I blame my sister. If she hadn't waited till I was 14 to arrive in the world, I might have learnt not to be so selfish in my conversations. I was the classic only child: indulged by my very loving parents and the focus of most of their attention. So I became accustomed to being the focus of other people's attention and, as a result, I expected other children to focus on me.

One way that I've found to make better connections with other people is to focus on those other people rather than focusing on myself. It was hard when I was feeling lonely. When I was living alone in a flat in London, for example, and I finally got a bit of company, I just wanted to talk so much that I monopolised the conversation. It wasn't dialogue – it was monologue. To really connect with someone, I realised far too late in life, you have to have a conversation. You have to listen and respond to what they say. It might sound obvious, but for many years, it wasn't obvious to me.

When I realised this and became aware of my conversation patterns, I beat myself up about it, thinking what an awful person I must have been, how inconsiderate and selfish. No wonder I didn't have any friends, I told myself. But many people do this. It wasn't just me. It's just something people do subconsciously. I've been trapped in corners by other people who do exactly the same thing as I used to do. They talk *at* me rather than *with* me.

129

These days I try to spend at least 50% of the time listening to the person I'm talking with. I try to respond to what *they're* saying: to nod, reply or best of all, ask follow-up questions. I try to move the focus away from me and my needs and try to focus on them – the chances of me having another conversation with that person are much higher as a result.

And of course, listening to someone else becomes infinitely easier if I am interested in them in the first place. Finding friends who share common interests with me makes the whole process a lot simpler.

2. Focus on being impressed rather than impressing someone

I mentioned my ego in the section on finding my authentic self. My ego often decides to surface when I'm meeting someone new and I start trying to impress them. I think that they'll like me if they know how many things I've achieved or what car I drive. Looking at the way people flock around celebrities and rich people these days, it seems a natural assumption to make.

But then I read that people don't like people they're impressed by. People like people who are impressed by them. So rather than telling them about my life and what I'm most proud of, I started trying to find out what other people are most proud of. It works. I've made some interesting friendships as a result.

3. Smile at strangers

Another tip from the *Making Slough Happy* programme was to smile at strangers.

I'm quite a serious person and when I'm thinking deeply about something, that thinking shows on my face. I pull a serious face. I haven't actually seen it myself – I don't usually look in a mirror when I'm thinking deeply – but I gather it's not a particularly pleasant or friendly face because friends always say, "What *are* you thinking about?"

I reckon I also pull this serious face when I'm at social gatherings and feeling anxious and nervous. It can't make me a very inviting prospect for new people to come up and talk to me. If I could only smile....

Smiling at strangers on the street is not only a way to feel connected, albeit in a small way, it's also a chance to practise smiling so that I get in the habit of being open and friendly when I meet new people. If I get in the habit of smiling as I'm walking about the place (though not in a contrived and slightly mad way) I might actually start smiling when I go to a party or event.

4. Ask for advice

My best friend always says that asking for advice is one of the easiest ways to cement a budding friendship. It's a safe way to allow someone to help you and when help is given in a relationship, it promotes trust in that relationship.

I couldn't immediately start asking new friends to help me move house or lend me money, but giving advice costs nothing. I don't make up situations simply to ask advice and I don't always follow the advice when I get it but friends seem flattered if I ask their advice – I suppose it shows that I value their opinion – and this really does seem to strengthen the connection with that person.

5. Build friendships

I used to mistakenly think that friendships just magically happened. You liked someone. They liked you. You became friends and lived happily ever after in a blissful socially embedded and connected world.

This just doesn't seem to be the case. Friendships do not just happen – at least, not in my life. One person usually has to take a step towards the other person – to issue that first invitation to go for a drink or to send that first text saying, "It was great meeting you at the party last night!"

Even when the initial contact has been made, when numbers have been swapped, when invitations have been issued, I have to work to keep friendships going. I have to be the person prepared to send that text when I haven't heard from someone in a while. I have to be prepared to

131

make time for a friend who needs a shoulder to cry on or to surrender the sofa for a few days for someone who needs somewhere to stay.

Some of my closest friendships are with people with whom I've deliberately sought to build a relationship. I didn't stalk them. I didn't pester them to be my friend until they gave in resignedly. I remembered their birthday, invited them for dinner and asked how their sick mother was or how their job interview had gone. Remembering the details of other people's lives doesn't always come easily to me. I really have to work at it. At one point, I even kept a notebook and recorded details of my friends' lives so I could more easily recall what I needed to remember to ask them next time I saw them.

Slowly, but surely, my friendships have developed over time. Sometimes, my efforts to make friends with someone haven't worked out. Texts never get replies, invitations get refused and no matter how much I like someone, I have to accept that either the feeling isn't mutual or they are too busy to have anyone new in their life. But the friendships that have developed have been well worth the effort. They've brought a great sense of connection into my life.

6. Expect the best of people

Psychologist John Cacioppo suggests that we should cultivate an "expect the best" attitude. This helps us to project warmth and goodwill and "warmth and goodwill on one person's part is more likely to elicit warmth and goodwill from other people—such is the power of reciprocity." It's not always easy to do that: when I've been feeling at my most lonely, it's difficult to turn up somewhere with an optimistic attitude. Normally I go thinking, "I expect no-one's going to speak to me. *Again.*"

The Dalai Lama tells us, in his book *The Art of Happiness,* that we should approach other people with the thought of compassion in order to "reduce fear and allow an openness with other people. It creates a positive, friendly atmosphere. With that attitude, you can approach a relationship in which you, yourself, initially create the possibility of receiving affection or a positive response from the other person….I think that in many cases people tend to expect the other person to respond to them in a positive way first, rather than taking the initiative themselves to create that possibility. I feel that's wrong; it leads to problems and can act as a barrier that just serves to promote that feeling of isolation from others. So if you wish to overcome those feelings of isolation and loneliness, I think that our underlying attitude makes a tremendous difference. And approaching others with the thought of compassion in your mind is the best way to do this."

7. Help people think big

Author Gretchen Rubin spent a year of her life in pursuit of more happiness. In June, her big goal was friendship and one of her top tips was to help other people to think big. "Words of enthusiasm and confidence from a friend can inspire you to tackle an ambitious goal," she says.

I think it does even more than that: it cements friendships. The friends I most like seeing, I've realised, are the ones who respond to my latest daft idea with comments like, "That's a great idea! I'd love to help!" So I try to respond to my friends' ideas with similar enthusiasm.

8. Use touch

According to the book *How to be Happy*, which accompanied the TV series *Making Slough Happy*, "studies have shown that just touching someone lightly on the arm makes it much more likely that they will respond to you in a more positive way." I've tried this and it works, though you have to be careful. Not everyone likes being touched, especially by someone they don't know and often this is more difficult with someone of the opposite sex. It's very easy to give the wrong impression.

9. Always wear a whatzit

"Always wear a whatzit," advises Leil Lowndes, author of *How to Talk To Anyone*. A whatzit, Leil explains, "is anything you wear of carry that is unusual –an interesting purse, a strange tie, an amusing hat. A whatzit is any object that draws people's attention and inspires them to approach you and ask, 'Uh, what's that?'"

"You can also be a Whatzit seeker," says Leil. "Become proficient in scrutinizing the apparel of those you wish to approach." Your whatzit is, apparently, a "crucial socialising artefact".

I don't consciously try to wear something unusual every time I go out, but I often admire someone's dress or coat and strike up a conversation that way. It's never led to a new friendship being developed, though I suppose it might if I met someone that way at a party, but it makes the other person feel good. Actually, paying compliments also makes *me* feel good.

I've had people on the street pay me compliments too, asking me where I'd bought my boots or handbag. In fact, a woman once stopped me and enquired where I'd had my hair done. I was extremely flattered – especially as I hadn't been to a hairdresser in months. Then I realised that she wasn't *admiring* my hairstyle but promoting a new salon and she'd simply clocked the fact that I was in need of a cut and colour.

In general though, wearing or carrying something that people can comment on and looking for what other people are wearing, carrying or even reading that I can comment on has proved a good way to strike up many a conversation.

10. Develop empathy

This, for me, was the crucial one. Empathy is being able to see things from someone else's point of view rather than just your own.

According to Daniel Menaker, author of *A Good Talk*, "…understanding what others are thinking and feeling – reading their minds, in a way – is crucial to successful personal interactions."

"When dealing with a person," advises the book *How to Win Friends and Influence People in the Digital Age*, a reworking of the Dale Carnegie classic, "always ask yourself, 'How would I feel, how would I react, if I were in his shoes?'…Once you take the time to consider the other person's perspective, you will become sympathetic to his feelings and ideas….Most people are merely looking for somebody who will listen to them and be sympathetic with their plight."

According to Dr. Raj Persaud in his book *Staying Sane*, how we assess the likelihood of making new friends can affect our levels of loneliness. If we feel optimistic about making new friendships in the future we'll feel less lonely than if we feel the opportunities for making friends has already passed us by in life.

As I improve my social skills, therefore, I don't just feel more confident around other people which in turn allows me to forge new social connections. I also feel more optimistic that I will be able to make even more new friends in the future, and that in itself is a good way to find freedom from loneliness.

Idea 31: Try internet dating

The dread of loneliness is greater than the fear of bondage,
so we get married.
~ Cyril Connolly

I hesitate to mention internet dating as an idea for helping loneliness. For a start, I realise that not every lonely person out there is single and not everyone's loneliness is caused by being single. When I was married, I still felt lonely because I felt a lack of connection to my husband. If I'm honest, that made me feel lonelier than being single ever has. One of my friends is very *happily* married but feels that she lacks a wider social network and therefore she still feels lonely. But I also hesitate to mention it because there have been times when internet dating has made me *more* lonely, not less lonely.

When I was first living on my own, just after my marriage broke down, I found it difficult to come home to an empty house after an evening out. Finding messages from guys I'd met on the internet really helped with this. I definitely felt less lonely if I arrived home to find the answer phone blinking and an email or two to reply to. On the other hand, in those first few difficult months, when I arrived home to find that the answer phone *wasn't* blinking and there were *no* emails, I felt lonelier than ever. I suppose it's similar to using technology in general: Facebook is great when you've received twenty messages, but it can feel like a really lonely place when no-one has contacted you at all.

The thing about internet dating is that it isn't 100% reliable. You can't count on the fact that you'll get messages. You might. You might not. And you might not get any dates.

"Technology changes our physical experiences of other people," say psychiatrists Jacqueline Olds and Richard Schwartz. "It changes how we think about our relationships …customers of online dating services go out with less than 1 per cent of people whose profiles they study, while participants on speed-dating events go out with more than one in ten of the people they meet."

So every time I spot a man on the internet whose photo I like enough to click through to his profile, there's a less than one per cent chance that I'll ever actually meet him. The trouble is that I get so excited when I see a profile I like and I get really disappointed when they don't send me a message back. The best way I've found of dealing with this is, to use Buddhist terminology, not to become too attached to the idea of getting messages, and especially not messages from one particular man. So if I get them, it's a bonus. If I don't, it doesn't matter. I try to cultivate this attitude of non-attachment, but in practice, I find it quite difficult.

Internet dating *can* be a great way of meeting people you wouldn't otherwise meet and having a bit of a social life at a time when things are feeling a bit flat. I know someone who gets so many dates that she can't fit them into her evenings and has to make dates in her lunch hour too. But I'm not sure if it really works as a way of finding a partner. The websites are full of stories of people who have found their soulmate through Match, Dating Direct or E-harmony but then they would say that wouldn't they? They want me to part with my cash. I dread to think how much I've spent on internet dating over the years and I'm *still* single.

I'm not sure if it really works for me – or for the majority of people - because it encourages a tick-list approach to making connections with people. If I meet someone at a party and I like them, I don't evaluate them according to a list of specified criteria before deciding whether I want to be friends with them or not. If I feel a sense of connection, if the conversation is interesting, if the feeling is mutual, I have made a new friend. It doesn't matter if they smoke, are under 5 foot 7 and haven't got a Masters degree. Yet on the internet, I find myself ticking boxes to say that I only want to meeting non-smoking graduates who are over 5 foot 8 and preferably don't have any children. This is what Jacqueline Olds and Richard

Schwartz call "an atmosphere of comparison shopping" and that atmosphere is not always "conducive to romance."

> When an introduction comes from a dating service or a personal ad, there is tremendous pressure on both individuals to make up their minds fast since the sole reason for the encounter is to decide if they are romantically interested in each other. Without a context that holds people together over time and permits them to reveal themselves to each other in a relaxed way, someone is more likely to make a snap judgment based on anxiety and fear.

But they do acknowledge that the internet has helped some of their loneliest patients.

> Online dating offers an increasingly important service in our social fragmented world...The power of the internet as a social universe is in its seemingly limitless possibilities. The trap of the internet as a social universe is also in its seemingly limitless possibilities. With limitless possibilities, why settle for any one of them? Something better might be just around the corner.

I've had that experience too – the "something better just around the corner" syndrome. I once met a man who seemed perfect for me. He was very attractive, funny *and* interesting and we had a wonderful first date, swiftly followed by a second. I arrived home after our second date to find he'd already sent a text: "I wish you could clone yourself and leave one copy here." Well, ok, a tad cheesy but I liked it at the time. I assumed, since he seemed so enthusiastic and I was too, that we would quickly embark on an exclusive relationship. Admittedly no mention was made of this, but we continued dating and I was just waiting for the words "exclusivity" or "relationship" to pop up in our conversations. And eventually they did. One day he told me that he *did* want an exclusive relationship – he just wanted it with one of the *other* women he'd been dating. I had assumed that neither of us was dating anyone else, since we had both admitted to liking each other pretty much from the word go. He was, however, dazzled by the limitless possibilities that internet dating offered and had indeed found something better just around the corner, as Olds and Schwartz put it.

Overall though, my experiences of internet dating have been positive. I have been doing internet dating now on and off for over seven years. I've made a couple of good male friends through it and even one female friend – she was a friend of a guy whom I dated for a little while and I met her at his birthday party. I also met my best friend through internet dating. Our relationship, though initially romantic, very quickly became platonic and then deepened into a very strong friendship and I wouldn't be without him for the world.

Idea 32: Help other people

You make a living by what you get. You make a life by what you give.
~ Winston Churchill

Search the books and websites offering advice to people with loneliness for a little while and before too long you're almost guaranteed to come across the word "volunteer".

John Cacioppo, psychologist and author of *Loneliness: Human Nature and the Need for Social Connection,* suggests that, as you take your first steps towards overcoming loneliness and venture into the world in search of social interactions, "you need a safe place to experiment…To improve your odds of eliciting a positive reaction—and to reduce your odds of being disappointed—you may want to confine your experimental outreach to the somewhat safer confines of charitable activities. Volunteer at a shelter or a hospice, teach elders how to use computers, tutor children, read to the blind, or help with a kids' sports team."

The Lonely Society, a report published in 2010 by the Mental Health Foundation, points out that, "Studies reveal that people who are engaged in service to others, such as volunteering, tend to be happier. Evolutionary psychologists point to evidence that altruism is an essential part of human nature, and that our focus on individual material wealth has obscured this."

As a song in my favourite musical *Avenue Q* says, "When you help others, you can't help helping yourself".

In the TV programme *Making Slough Happy,* "Spread some kindness - do a good turn for someone every day" was one of the ten steps in the "Happiness Manifesto". Author Liz Hoggard, who wrote the book that accompanies the series, points out that "Volunteering in a good cause gives us as much happiness as doubling our income. Those who do so even live longer….We establish deep interpersonal relationships and empathy for others, and also have the perfect opportunity to practise flow activities – those things we enjoy and that really take us out of ourself....It makes us feel generous and capable and gives us a greater sense of connection with others."

There's loads of ways to volunteer too. The websites *Do-It* and *Timebank* offer plenty of volunteering opportunities or you can go along to your local volunteer centre. Volunteering then seems like the perfect solution to loneliness – you can do something useful *and* make new friends at the same time.

But it isn't quite the quick fix it appears to be. One of my first forays into the world of volunteering was to befriend a lonely elderly person by visiting her on a regular basis. I thought that this would be ideal: surely the best sort of volunteering for me *would* be to help someone suffering from loneliness. I hadn't foreseen that we wouldn't get on.

I wasn't in a particularly happy place in my life at the time, and having to spend an afternoon every week talking to someone I didn't really connect with made my happiness levels slump, rather than rise. What's more, this particular form of volunteering meant that the only new person I met was the old person in question. Eventually, I admitted that I couldn't continue with the visits. I felt bad about it, but I was starting to *dread* those afternoon visits and I couldn't carry on.

I felt even worse about it when I read on author Emily White's blog that: "Studies show that isolated elderly people actually do *worse* if a friendly visitor shows up for, say, three months, and then disappears. Friendly visiting is a much bigger commitment than the websites offering 'advice' make it out to be. If you really care about social isolation and the elderly, and if there's a seniors' advocacy center in your city, then think about it. But be ready to *commit.*"

Finding a volunteer centre where you can work as part of a team is a much safer idea. At my local food drop-in centre, at least 20 volunteers arrive each week, to package up and give out food parcels or simply provide a listening ear to those in need. It's sociable and friendly and it doesn't matter if there's a week when you can't show up. There are so many people that the centre will still run smoothly anyway.

But sometimes, the whole process of volunteering can be a bit frustrating. I've filled in tons of forms that I've never had a reply to. I've been to training sessions with a local homeless project but never been offered any actual volunteer work. I've been on a fundraising committee that never organized any fundraising events and just consisted of one committee meeting after another (though I have to admit that the meetings were quite sociable as they were held in pubs!) As a professional TV producer, I thought that charities would welcome me with open arms if I offered to make free films for them. I wrote to several charities but only one took me up on my offer. Having said that, I made good friends on that filming trip to Uganda and even received an invitation to the Houses of Parliament as a result.

The key to volunteering seems to be to find something that fits in with my interests and lifestyle. It's the same principle as I try to apply when joining a club. I wouldn't join a club that offered an activity that I didn't enjoy just because I wanted to meet new people. I try to find clubs that offer things that I already like. I like walking and I like dogs, but I don't like the hassle of picking up poo or having my arms wrenched out of their sockets, so volunteering to walk dogs at the local rescue centre wouldn't be my cup of tea. But I like wildlife, so I did volunteer to be warden, though it was yet another form that I filled in and got no response to. But by volunteering for something that I am really interested in doing, when it *does* come off, I end up not just enjoying the volunteering work itself more, but meeting people who have similar interests to mine, thereby making it more likely that I'll make new friends and increase my sense of connection.

Idea 33: Make a song and dance of it

Music can induce some of the deepest
experiences of sharing and connection.
~ Jacqueline Olds and Richard Schwartz

I stumbled on Ceroc dancing a few weeks after my ex-husband and I went our separate ways. The ending of the marriage had also effectively ended my social life – most of the people we'd socialised with had been *his* friends. I had a few friends in the office but I didn't see them much outside work. I literally didn't know what to do with my evenings and my weekends and loneliness began to set in.

I'd enjoyed dancing as a child, going to weekly ballet classes, but had never done any as an adult. I've never been into discos or nightclubs. But I saw a Ceroc dancing workshop advertised. It was fairly inexpensive, near my home and would take up an entire Sunday morning and afternoon. I think I would have done almost anything at the time if it took up a Sunday – it was my most miserable day of the week in those first few months of being alone.

I was hooked from the start. Ceroc is like a mixture of jive and salsa, but actually I'm not sure that it mattered too much what the dance was actually like. What mattered was that everyone else there was single, the steps were easy and it was sociable. I was hooked. Best of all, in my local area, there was at least one class every single night of the week that I could go to, and I could show up on my own – you didn't need to bring a partner.

Pretty soon, I'd bought proper dance shoes and was going 3 or 4 times a week. I soon made friends. I soon became reasonably good at the steps. I even lost weight. Each class began with a beginners' lesson, covering 4 of the basic moves. The men lined up and the women found a partner. The resulting couples made lines down the room and every two or three minutes, the women would move round, onto the next man in the line, so that everyone got a

143

chance to dance with everyone else. There was no question of being left out. There were then twenty minutes or so of freestyle, when they put on music and you danced with whoever you wanted. Then it was the intermediate class and the chance to learn some more difficult moves before another hour or more of freestyle. The whole evening lasted till half past ten or sometimes eleven o'clock and I'd come home exhausted but happy.

It wasn't just the dancing. I loved the music – it could be anything. Chart music, blues music, old fashioned show tunes, faster jive numbers. I didn't realise that I'd unwittingly stumbled upon something that social psychologists have proven to be key ingredients in the quest for happiness. According to *How to Be Happy*, the book which accompanied the TV series *Making Slough Happy*: "The late pioneering social psychologist Michael Argle, who conducted numerous happiness studies, showed that among the things that make people happy are sport, music and – best of all dancing…Group dancing, which combines exercise, music, community, touch and rules, also dramatically increases happiness."

I'd also unwittingly stumbled upon the concept of flow. Flow is a mental state described by psychology professor Mihály Csíkszentmihályi as "being completely involved in an activity for its own sake. The ego falls away. Time flies. Every action, movement, and thought follows inevitably from the previous one, like playing jazz. Your whole being is involved, and you're using your skills to the utmost." When I was dancing, I couldn't focus on anything *but* dancing. I had to focus, to concentrate on the steps. I couldn't be worrying about going home to an empty house or what I was going to do at the weekend or whether the divorce would go through smoothly.

Music is, for me and many others, another way to find flow. The first job I ever had was as a music teacher, so I'm bound to speak up for the therapeutic powers of listening to music. One of the 12 steps to happiness recommended in *How to Be Happy* is "Listen to music. It's both relaxing and stimulating and can also boost your brainpower." For me, it's Saint-Saëns' magnificent organ symphony – it always lifts my spirits. My most miserable of moods evaporates when I hear it.

But making music is even better than listening to it. In *Making Slough Happy,* psychotherapist Brett Kahr, who also happens to be an accomplished musician and composer, got participants singing in a group choir. The members of the "happiness choir" seemed sceptical at first. Some had never sung a note in their lives. Memories of terrible school music lessons clearly still haunted some of them. But almost everyone was converted by the end of the series.

I witnessed a similar delight in the faces of an opera group at the Connection, a centre for homeless people based at the Church of St Martin-in-the-Fields in Trafalgar Square. Thankfully, I can't speak from personal experience, but being homeless must surely be desperately lonely and isolating. Yet at an open day at the centre, the participants were full of joy as they sang choruses from various operas. Perhaps it wasn't just the satisfaction of making music but the experience of making music *together.*

Dr. Frederick Tims led a team of researchers for a University of Miami Alzheimer's project on music therapy. A group of 61 retired people took keyboard lessons over two 10-week semesters. A similar sized group of retired people did not take keyboard lessons, to act as a control. Various aspects of the participants' health were measured at intervals throughout the trial. Levels of anxiety and depression were found to decrease in the keyboard group but not the control group. Most interesting to me though was the fact that the levels of loneliness also decreased in the keyboard group, whilst they remained the same in the control group. Perhaps it's time to get that old keyboard out of the loft or bring the flute that I played as a teenager out of hibernation!

145

Idea 34: Find sociable work

It is an absolute bonus to make friends out of colleagues
~ Jennifer Aniston

I went through a bad patch recently. I thought that I'd got the better of my loneliness – that I'd cured myself, that I'd put all my loneliness ideas into action and that I was free of it at last. But a combination of a potential new relationship not going too well and an empty diary – all my closest friends happened to be busy at the same time - left me desolate. I spent evening after evening, slumped on the sofa, feeling downright miserable and wishing that I had someone to spend my time with.

At the time, I was between jobs, working as a supply teacher for the local education authority. This job seemed great for me: it offered a fairly regular income but also the flexibility of being able to take a day off here and there to focus on some of my other projects. It was ideal. Or that's what I thought.

One day, arriving home to find me more miserable than ever, my housemate made a rather insightful observation. Most people, he said, get a certain amount of sociability from their job. Even if they aren't going out with their colleagues every evening, even if they aren't "best mates" with other people in the office, there's still the daily banter of "How was your weekend?" or "Did you see the *X Factor* final?" My days, he observed, consisted either of staying at home all alone if my services weren't needed by the local education authority or of parachuting into a strange new school, where I knew no-one and where no-one ever bothered to include me in their lunchtime conversations.

Not having a regular workplace – or frequently working on short-term contracts and having to change jobs so that you always feel like the new girl (or boy) - can really exacerbate loneliness. You just never get chance to make connections at work. You're never there long enough.

My last full-time, long-term job – working in a TV company - offered me loads of opportunities to socialise. It was a particularly sociable office. It was fantastic walking in every morning to find people telling me what they'd done the night before or asking me to go out for a drink after work. There were always people to talk to and friendships were easily formed. Sometimes I wonder how we ever got any work done. But those connections that I forged with my colleagues played a big part in keeping my loneliness at bay.

A sociable workplace becomes even more important as we work longer and longer hours. Time is a fixed commodity. If my working hours get longer, I have less time to spend with my friends and family. Not only that, but after a long day at work, I'm just too tired to want to spend the time that I *have* got free doing anything other than vegging out on the sofa. If I'm going to spend more time at work, it stands to reason that I will be less lonely if I work somewhere sociable and can make friends there. In other words, if the current employment market demands that I spend more time at work in order to stay in employment, making social connections *at* work becomes even more important.

Working in a sociable office and having colleagues who are friends rather than just colleagues is great. But, whenever I move on to another job, when I've been made redundant or when my short-term contract has simply finished, the end of my job has often meant the end of my friendships. My chosen industry, working in television, has never been the most stable of working environments, but sadly, in these difficult economic times, it's more likely than ever that I'll be made redundant, or that I'll find myself working in a series of short-term positions. When I leave a job, it takes more than a bit of effort to keep up with the new friends that I've made there.

I knew, when I made the decision to leave that really sociable office in the TV company, that the

147

friendships that I'd made there rather easily, would also be easily lost. I knew when I made the decision to leave, that I would no longer have much contact with people from the office and that a big hole would be left in my social life. There was one person in particular whom I felt sorry to say goodbye to. She was a great colleague and we'd shared some personal things about ourselves on the long car journeys that the nature of our work sometimes necessitated. So I made a decision: I would actively nurture that friendship. A week or so after I left, I asked her if she fancied meeting up. She's the only person from that office whom I still see on a regular basis.

These days, when I'm not supply teaching, I'm working as a freelance video producer. This means working from home and working mainly alone. With the advent of modern technology, more and more people are able to work from home. Whilst it's great not to have to sit in traffic for hours on the daily commute, in terms of loneliness, working from home is far from ideal for me.

Whether I work from home, work short-term contracts or work in a sociable office, the place where I'm working has a big influence on whether or not I feel lonely. But I don't always have a choice, especially as unemployment figures currently seem to be rising all the time. Sometimes, like many people, I find myself having to accept jobs that aren't ideal for me. But when I do find myself in the enviable position of having a choice about my job and working environment, I'll be taking the loneliness factors into consideration before making any decisions.

Idea 35: Read all about it

Be careful about reading health books. You may die of a misprint.
~ Mark Twain

I feel a real sense of connection when I learn about other people who have felt lonely or about how people have gone off to live on their own and discovered a great sense of contentment in their solitude. Finding out about other people's experiences of loneliness and solitude is a great comfort. Initially, I didn't feel able to "come out" as lonely to my friends and family and ask them if they ever felt lonely. Until I did feel ready, reading was a great substitute.

Sometimes, I must admit, I was embarrassed as I handed over books with one of the "L" words – *lonely* or *loneliness* - in the title to the librarian in my local library. I wondered if she was judging me for wanting to read such a book, if she had guessed that I was lonely too. To be honest, I'd have felt less embarrassed borrowing *Frigidity: An Intellectual History* or the *Encyclopaedia of Sexually Transmitted Diseases*. I wished I'd gone and bought it on Amazon instead, so that it would have arrived in an anonymous little brown package.

But my embarrassment disappeared as I opened the covers and started reading. Here were people who felt just like I did.

There are plenty of books out there that detail other people's personal journeys through loneliness, silence and solitude. *Lonely: A Memoir* by Emily White is a book I'd definitely recommend, along with Sean Seepersad's book *The Lonely Screams. Celebrating Time Alone: Stories of Splendid Solitude* is a collection of real-life stories from people who've spent time living in solitude. Their experiences are interwoven with the personal reflections of author, Lionel Fisher, who lived alone for six years on a remote beach. *Singled Out* by Virginia Nicholson tells the story of the 2 million women whose chances of marriage were almost obliterated when nearly three-quarters of a million men were slaughtered in the atrocities of the First World War.

In *A Book of Silence,* author Sara Maitland tells of her experiments with silence - Zen meditation, a flotation tank, a week in the Sinai Desert and her six-week retreat on the Isle of Skye. She then relates the story of her subsequent move to live alone in silence on a more permanent basis, first on the Durham Moors and then in south-west Scotland.

Writer Alice Koller once said, "Being solitary is being alone well: being alone luxuriously immersed in doings of your own choice, aware of the fullness of your own presence rather than of the absence of others. Because solitude is an achievement." Her books, *An Unknown Woman* and *The Stations of Solitude,* are well worth reading.

Finally, I love *Eat Pray Love,* Elizabeth Gilbert's story of her spiritual, year-long journey through Italy, India and Bali, which begins with a lonely night crying on her bathroom floor.

There's one book that I have to confess that I haven't read yet, but which is top of my "must read" list, a book that keeps popping up in almost every other book I've read as I've researched my loneliness solutions: *Walden* by Henry David Thoreau. Thoreau considered that we were *too* much in contact with one another, that "society is commonly too cheap" and he took himself off to live in a cabin by a lake. I wonder what he'd make of today's world of Facebook, Twitter and constant texting on mobile phones.

It's not just true stories that bring me comfort and a sense of solace. I love *The Knitting Circle,* by Ann Hood, which tells the story of a group of women, all struggling with different heartaches, who are brought together by knitting.

Sometimes, I take comfort from a book, finding someone whose struggles with loneliness seem to mirror my own. And sometimes, as in the case of *A Book of Silence,* I find inspiration, the hope that even if I continue on my journey through life alone, I can still find ways for that aloneness to be rich, meaningful and even full of contentment.

Idea 36: Understand how social networks work

*We're born alone, we live alone, we die alone. Only through our love
and friendship can we create the illusion for the moment
that we're not alone.*
~ Orson Welles

A social network is a theoretical construct, something that social scientists use as a way of understanding how social relationships interact with each other.

I wanted to understand how social networks function because I wondered whether the social networks that I'm in play a role somehow in whether or not I'm feeling lonely. I had an inkling that I do not exist in a little bubble but am affected by the feelings and actions of other people. Social networks function through people forming connections with each other and perhaps the quality and quantity of connections in *my* social networks play a role in my levels of loneliness.

According to Nicholas Christakis and James Fowler, two American doctors who wrote the book *Connected: The Amazing Power of Social Networks and How They Shape Our Lives*, our actions and our state of mind can affect not only those people we know, but people we have never met. "We discovered," they write, "that if your friend's friend's friend gained weight, you gained weight... And we discovered if your friend's friend's friend became happy, you became happy."

Christakis and Fowler found that feelings of loneliness could disseminate throughout a social network in the same way as feelings of happiness appeared to spread. "A person's loneliness depends not only on his friends' loneliness, but also on his friends' friends' and his friends' friends' friends' loneliness. The full network shows that you are about 52 per cent more likely to be lonely if a person you are directly connected to (at one degree of separation) is lonely."

Christakis and Fowler's research revealed that loneliness is both a consequence of becoming disconnected from the network – i.e. having fewer connections – and a cause. They observed that people who felt chronically lonely tended to lose their friends. Those with fewer friends were likely to be lonelier and that feeling made it less likely that they would seek and form new friendships. In other words, loneliness seemed to be self-perpetuating. If you're lonely, you feel trapped in a vicious circle: you desperately need to make new connections with other people but your feelings of loneliness seem to prevent you from doing so.

The most extraordinary finding though was at the edge of the social network. "At the periphery," observe Christakis and Fowler, "people have fewer friends; this makes them lonely, but also tends to drive them to cut the few ties that they have left. But before they do, they may infect their friends with the same feeling of loneliness, starting the cycle anew. These reinforcing effects mean that our social fabric can fray at the edges, like a strand of yarn that comes loose from the sleeve of a sweater. If we are concerned about combating the feeling of loneliness in our society, we should aggressively target the people at the periphery with interventions to repair their social networks. By helping them, we can create a protective barrier against loneliness that will keep the whole network from unraveling."

I'm not sure I fancy being the object of "obsessive targeting" but I am aware that sometimes I *have* been like that fraying yarn, coming loose from the network and paradoxically wanting to sever ties at times when I was feeling most in need of connections. If I don't want to become disconnected from the networks that I'm in, I realise, I have to fight those feelings of wanting to break loose in the first place, thereby protecting myself against becoming lonelier.

Idea 37: Seek quality not quantity

What loneliness is more lonely than distrust?
~ T.S. Eliot

In recent years, I've made a big effort to find sociable things to do. As a consequence I have a busy social life and I've been going out most evenings as well as at the weekends. I have a lot of social interaction in my life and more friends than I've ever had.

"Most of us have an average of 30 friends at any one time," says Liz Hoggard, author of *How to Be Happy,* "Over a lifetime, we make around 400 friends, but just 10 per cent of those will last."

Reading this, I realise that I'm lucky enough, at the moment at least, to have *more* than the average number of friends. Yet I still feel lonely sometimes.

Sometimes, I can be with a group of people and I feel much lonelier than when I'm alone. I just don't feel that sense of connection with the people I'm with. Meeting up with a friend for a coffee doesn't always take the edge off my loneliness: sometimes I leave feeling lonelier than ever.

"Paradoxically," Dr Raj Persaud observes in his book *Staying Sane,* "some people who appear to have few friends may be less lonely than those who seem very popular, if the former can turn to their friends at times of crisis and confide things which would be socially unacceptable to reveal to mere acquaintances."

I've realised that it's not just the amount of social interaction that I have in my life that determines whether or not I feel lonely. The amount doesn't seem to matter. It's the quality of the interaction that counts.

One friend told me that, for her, loneliness is "being in the wrong relationship where all communication has died; being in a group situation where you don't really bond with who is there; at work where you are the new girl/boy and not really included in anything; being at a

154

works 'do' without a partner when everyone else has taken one. Loneliness is not being alone. You can feel lonely when you are with your friends."

I have a handful of friends whom I'd consider "best friends" and meeting up with them never leaves me feeling lonely. We never struggle for something to say. Even if we haven't seen each other for a while, we somehow manage to pick up where we left off.

At other times, I'll meet up with other friends – people whom I like but don't consider as close friends. Sometimes, I'll have a great time. We'll go out dancing. We'll go out for a meal. The conversation – and the wine – flow. But at other times, particularly for me in a group scenario, I'll meet up with friends and feel more isolated than if I'd stayed home alone with my boxed set of Downton Abbey DVDs.

The depth of connection just isn't always there. Of course, this is also very subjective and difficult to define, but it's also borne out by scientific research. Social psychologist John Cacioppo's research showed that "it isn't the number of contacts or the frequency of interaction with other people, it's the quality of those interactions."

I probably shouldn't admit this in case any of my friends are actually reading this and I then end up with less friends when they take offence, but mentally, I have kind of categorized my friends into "A list", "B list" and "C list" type friends and so on – the way celebrities get categorized by the gossip magazines. I admit this mightn't be the nicest thing to do, but it doesn't mean that I like people less or consider them less valuable as people. It might be that I would love for one of my "C list" friends to be an "A list" friend but I know that *they* don't necessarily want that close friendship with me. This categorisation is useful: I know that in the interests of my emotional well-being, I need to make sure that I leave room in my diary for my "A list" friends. My "B list" and "C list" friends are great fun and I love seeing them, but it's seeing my "A list" friends that gives me that deep sense of connection and staves off loneliness.

One of the characteristics, one of the most important characteristics, of those close friendships is trust.

Nothing makes me feel lonelier than being let down by someone. I've arranged to go for a drink with someone but then they ring at the last minute to say they can't make it. They don't give a reason. There are some people who always seem to cancel and some people who are always late: another thing that makes me feel lonely as it makes me feel I'm not important to someone. One "friend" once confessed that she often arranged three things to do every evening. She might agree to meet a friend for a drink, go to the cinema with another friend and go to a party. She did this because she was so afraid that *she* would be let down and left lonely. Having a choice of three activities gave her some security – the chances of all three things being cancelled were slim. Unfortunately, this usually meant that she was letting other people down – she was always fixing to do things with me and then cancelling at the last minute. Once I realised about her triple-booking policy, I stopped arranging to meet her. I was fed up of being let down. I felt she disappeared if she got a better offer and I didn't feel I could trust her.

My experience of lonely feelings being triggered by relationships with people I felt I couldn't trust is borne out by academic findings. Ken Rotenberg of Keele University carried out studies of non-lonely and lonely individuals and discovered that there was some correlation between people's levels of loneliness and their beliefs about other people's reliability – or unreliability as the case may be.

But lack of trust is not the only thing that seems to affect some of my friendships. Having unspoken and different expectations about the level of contact with someone has also had a detrimental effect on some of my relationships with other people, particularly people of the opposite sex.

I discussed this with a friend very recently. She thought she'd done something to offend me because she hadn't had a text from me in what she described as "ages". When we actually compared our phones, it had only been 4 days and it had been a very busy 4 days for me. Her expectation – and mine too usually – was that close friends like me would text her every couple of days at the very least to see that she was ok. The lack of texts was perceived as lack of caring and she felt anxious about our friendship.

I've felt this too on occasion, when I've been expecting to hear from someone and I haven't. I've felt let down, as *if* I couldn't trust them but actually no arrangement had been made. They hadn't been one of those people who'd fixed up to see me and then cancelled. The expectation to hear from them was purely in my head. It was an unspoken expectation. I'm sure the person concerned would have been surprised to hear that I'd felt let down: they probably had no idea how I was feeling. "The problem," my housemate advises me, "is that you expect other people to behave like you. You text everyone the minute you arrive back from your holidays, so you expect your friends to do the same, and then you're upset when you don't hear from them. But they might prefer to unpack and sleep off their jetlag first."

Making more friends has really helped me fight off loneliness. I'm trying to make sure I allow time in my weekly schedule to see my closest friends. I understand how important trust is in those close relationships so I'm careful not to let people down, and to avoid too much involvement with people who repeatedly let me down. And I'm trying to be aware of my own often unrealistic expectations. Hopefully that will ensure that I don't just have friends, I continue to have *close* friends, because it seems that when it comes to friendships and loneliness, it's definitely quality more than quantity that makes the difference.

Idea 38: Write letters

Letter writing is the only device for combining solitude with good company.
~ Lord Byron

I was a bit of a solitary child growing up. I had a best friend at school, but if we fell out (and we frequently did!) I was usually left with no-one to play with. My best friend didn't live particularly near me either, so I couldn't just pop round to her house after school. In fact, I didn't have any friends who lived in our village that I could just pop round and see. I was an only child too, until I was 14, when my sister finally arrived.

But throughout this lonely childhood, I always had pen pals. My best pen pal was called Susilla and she lived in London, which seemed very exotic to a northern girl like me. I came across her through an advert in a magazine for junior members of the RSPCA and I think we were about 9 when we started writing to each other. We wrote for many years and my best friend at school started writing to *Susilla's* best friend at school. The four of us once went on holiday to the Sussex coast with her parents. We sadly lost touch in our mid-teens: I think our interests had gone in different directions by then. But those years of writing to Susilla certainly helped my childhood to feel a little less lonely.

Throughout my teenage years, I wrote to Didier in France in order to practise my French. I enjoyed writing to Dider, *and* I managed to scrape an A at 'O' Level.

There's a box in the loft full of my old letters from various people. I went to university abroad and phone calls back to England were expensive. I used to speak to my parents once a week, but in the meantime my dad would write to me. Those letters are in that box and they're such a beautiful record of my relationship with my father. I have letters from old boyfriends too – one collection still smells vaguely of the aftershave Kouros. He used to spray his letters! I have letters from my auntie Joan whom I hardly ever met but felt like I knew through our correspondence. I love that box: opening it is like delving into a treasure trove of memories.

I have a pen pal now too. I found him through an organisation called Lifelines: he is a prisoner on Death Row in the United States. I started writing to him because I wanted to do something charitable, but I have to admit that the friendship helps me at least as much, if not more, than it helps him. If I've nothing to do and no-one to be with over a weekend, and loneliness is starting to creep in, I pick up a pen and write to him and I feel as if I've got company, as if I'm having a really deep conversation with a really close friend.

Well, he *has* become a close friend and we *do* have really deep conversations and the fact that they're written conversations rather than spoken ones doesn't seem to change the fact that they ease my sense of loneliness. The conversations that I have with him are *very* deep indeed: he's spent his years in prison reading Camus, Plato and Sartre and we discuss everything from my lack of love life to the meaning of life.

Because of email, we're in danger of becoming the generation that didn't leave letters behind for future generations to enjoy. If email had been around 150 years earlier, there'd have been no letters from Vincent Van Gogh to his brother Theo, for example. So many figures through history have left us letters: Napoleon, Jane Austen, Elizabeth Barrett Browning and Robert Browning, to name but a few.

Much as I love getting emails, there is still nothing quite like the thrill of hearing the postman dropping an envelope through the door and realising that it's not a bill but a real letter from a real person. But although the advent of email seems to have been a nail in the coffin of the art of letter-writing, using the internet could actually make it easier to find a pen pal. Do a Google search and there are plenty of websites offering to set you up with a good old-fashioned pen pal. Visit the website of the Sun newspaper, for example, and agony aunt Deirdre will find you a pen pal in the armed forces.

It seems I am not the only one who likes getting letters. The American arts magazine, *The Rumpus,* recently started a new initiative with a group of writers, headed up by Dave Eggers, author of *A Heartbreaking Work of Staggering Genius.* Readers can sign up to receive one letter a week from different writers including Eggers himself, Tao Lin, Stephen Elliott, Emily Gould and Jonathan Ames. "Think of it as the letters you used to get from your creative friends, before this whole internet/email thing," says the Rumpus. "Most of the letters will include return addresses (at the author's discretion) in case you want to write the author back." Over a thousand people signed up immediately and the number is still growing.   Award-winning American author and puppeteer, Mary Robinette Kowal took a month off the internet in September 2011. She told people that they could correspond with her only by writing paper letters and many people did. Mary says that writing letters is a different thing altogether from writing emails.

When I write back, I find that I slow down and write differently than I do with an email. Email is all about the now. Letters are different, because whatever I write needs to be something that will be relevant a week later to the person to whom I am writing. In some ways it forces me to think about time more because postal mail is slower. *'By the time you get this…'* It is relaxing. It is intimate. It is both lasting and ephemeral. How so? I find that I will often read the letters that I receive twice. Once when I get them and again as I write back. So, that makes it more lasting. It is more ephemeral because I don't have copies of the letters that I write and I am the only one who has copies of the letters that my correspondents write. So, more ephemeral.

In February 2012, Mary set the readers of her blog a challenge: to mail at least one item through the post every day. The challenge ran for the entire month. Participants could send postcards, letters, pictures, cuttings from a newspaper or even fabric swatches and they also had to write back to everyone who had written to them. The challenge generated a huge amount of interest, with almost 20,000 people visiting Mary's website.

Mary Robinette Kowal and the group of writers at *The Rumpus* are not the only ones who are reviving the lost art of writing letters. Louis Schlamowitz, an elderly Jewish man who lives in Brooklyn, has spent decades of his life writing to world leaders. He's corresponded with JFK, Ayatollah Khomeini and the recently deceased Colonel Gaddafi.

Louis has 60 albums full of letters and signed pictures and his walls are decorated with photos from many of them, including a shot of Louis meeting President Richard Nixon at the White House. The letter writing began in 1953 when he was in Korea with the US Army. A friend suggested that he used a spare Christmas card to write to President Harry Truman. Truman replied, and Louis started researching the birthdays and anniversaries of public figures in order to send them cards too.

"I feel good when they write back," says Louis. "I'm nothing special, just an ordinary guy, and now I'm part of history."

Letter writing is an alternative way to connect with other people, when the opportunities for face-to-face connection are limited. The benefits of writing letters are well-documented, but you don't have to actually send a letter in order to reap those benefits. Letter writing can also provide a way of connecting with your own feelings and emotions.

At times when I've been struggling with my emotions, getting them down on paper has been very therapeutic. Usually I do that in my journal, but sometimes I've found it very healing to write a letter to someone who has hurt me in the past. It enables me to confront

161

unresolved feelings and fears. I don't actually *post* these letters. I'm not writing to let the person know how I feel but simply to acknowledge those feelings to myself – to get them into the open. I've written, for example, to a woman who made my life a nightmare in my first ever full-time job and whose actions made me feel alienated and excluded. I've written to my ex-husband about some of the things he did that I was unhappy about but never dared broach in our marriage. I've written to my ex-boss about his bullying attitude and told him how he made me feel. Except I didn't *actually* tell him. I ripped the letter up, and threw it away, trying to let go of my feelings about that past situation as I did.

One of my favourite books, *The Artists' Way,* advocates writing letters to yourself *from* yourself, perhaps imagining, for example, what your 80-year-old self would say to your current self. Author Joseph Galliano had a similar idea: his book *Dear Me* includes letters from well-known personalities such as Stephen Fry, Annie Lennox, Fay Weldon, Sir Ranulph Fiennes and Yoko Ono, all writing to their sixteen year old selves.

I actually tried this. Once I got started, it was pretty easy to imagine what my eighty year old self might say to my current self if she could write a letter back through history: stop looking for Mr Right and just enjoy your life whilst you can!

Idea 39: Visit and be visited

Every woman needs to have friends who drop in for tea or cocktails or supper, and who ask her to drop in.
~ Marjorie Hillis, Live Alone and Like It

When I first read Emily White's book *Lonely: A Memoir*, I was struck by this statistic: the British Social Attitudes Survey, comparing data from 1986 and 1995, found that weekly visits with parents had fallen by 10%, with siblings and other relatives by between 3% and 7% and with friends by 6%. It seems that we are less likely to visit and be visited.

According to Emily White, as family sizes have decreased, there's been an "increased emphasis on 'active socialising'"- in other words, people tend to meet in coffee shops or restaurants or go to events like sports fixtures and music gigs, rather than visiting each other at home.

> As we find ourselves increasingly on our own, we try to offset that aloneness by setting up get-togethers with others….there's nothing wrong with indulging in a high-fat latte with a friend, but there are a few problems associated with it. First, the shift towards active socialising will inevitably exclude those who don't have any discretionary income, and who can't afford not just a high-end latte but even a coffee at a greasy spoon….What people who are lonely want isn't yet another cocoa with whipped cream, but rather a sense of connection that's present, lasting and strong.

I realized, as I read this, that this was true of my life. I *never* invited anyone to my house for a meal or even a cup of tea. The neighbours never just pop in for a quick coffee and a cuppa. As my father has got older, he finds stairs difficult to manage and we only have an upstairs bathroom, so even my parents don't visit any more. I hardly

163

ever visit anyone either. I always meet my friends on neutral ground, usually a pub that's half way between my place and theirs.

What if I reversed the trend of visiting patterns in my own life? Could I, I wondered, offset some of my feelings of loneliness? ? Could it really be that meeting in Costa Coffee wasn't as effective at combating loneliness as meeting at a friend's house or inviting them round to my place?

Surprisingly, the answer seemed to be yes. Once I started inviting friends over for coffee or a meal or inviting myself over to their place, I *did* feel less lonely.

I felt less anxious about socialising too. Meeting in a bar or a pub sometimes makes me a little nervous. The timing has to be just right. I don't like being late, but if I arrive too early, I end up sitting on my own, nursing a drink, worrying that I look like Billy-No-Mates. Arrival times are difficult to judge too: there's the problem of finding a parking space for a start – not always easy in a city like Manchester or Leeds. Meeting at a friend's house removes that hassle.

You can get cosier at someone's home than you can in a pub. You can put your feet up (well, I put *my* feet up at my friends' houses!) and it's more relaxed somehow.

Offering hospitality – and accepting the hospitality of going to another person's home rather than a pub or a restaurant – really does seem to strengthen my sense of connection to my friends.

According to writer Henri Nouwen, "The first characteristic of the spiritual life is the continuing movement from loneliness to solitude. Its second equally important characteristic is the movement by which our hostilities can be converted into hospitality. It is there that our changing relationship to ourself can be brought to fruition in an ever-changing relationship to our fellow human beings."

PART 4:
DEVELOP A
CONNECTION WITH
GOD

Idea 40: Pray or meditate

Pray that your loneliness may spur you into finding
something to live for, great enough to die for.
~ Dag Hammarskjöld

I've discovered that prayer helps loneliness. Even at times of doubt, when I'm not sure whether God really is listening or whether he's even there, praying eases my loneliness. I am not sure who I am talking to or whether I'm talking to anyone other than myself, but I feel a sense of connection when I pray.

I was hesitant about writing about a connection with God. My faith in God is a private affair and I have no desire to "convert" others to share it. I do not want anyone to be put off continuing to read by my mention of the word "God".

But praying, meditating and, as I suggest in Idea 41, learning to enjoy silence all help you to find a connection. Perhaps, if you have a religious faith, that connection is a connection with God. But if you don't, it might be a deeper connection to your inner self.

"Your treasure is within you," says the inspirational writer and priest Gerard W. Hughes. "It takes most of us a long time and we have many obstacles to overcome before we begin to recognise the field where our treasure is hidden, that is, before we find and accept ourselves, where God is. Until we do find ourselves, God remains a remote, shadowy figure, to some unimportant, to others terrifying."

In her best-selling book *Eat Pray Love,* writer Elizabeth Gilbert suggests that God "does not live in a dogmatic scripture or in a distant throne in the sky, but instead abides very close to us indeed – much closer than we can imagine."

At times in my life, I have found the word "God" a difficult word to use. But during those times, I still believed

166

in something. Julia Cameron suggests, in *The Artists Way*, that you don't refer to God "unless it is comfortable for you." Her alternative suggestions include Goddess, Mind, Universe, Source and Higher Power.

I don't worry about what God is called. I call him God because I'd label myself a Christian, if forced to use a label at all. In reality I find that most religious traditions have something worthwhile to offer. As usual in my life, I am being a jack of all trades and master of none, and failing to commit to one single path. I've tried Buddhist meditation, Christian churches, Quaker meetings and even the occasional visit to a Sikh gurdwara.

Elizabeth Gilbert puts it much better than I can: "In the end, what I have come to believe about God is simple. It's like this – I used to have this really great dog. She came from the pound. She was a mixture of about ten different breeds but seemed to have inherited the finest features of all of them. She was brown. When people asked me, 'What kind of dog is that?' I would always give the same answer, 'She's a brown dog.' Similarly, when the question is raised, 'What kind of God do you believe in?' my answer is easy: 'I believe in a magnificent God.'"

Taking part in organised religion, praying, meditating and spending time being silent have all brought me freedom from loneliness. But I'm not always sure how to start praying. I was once told by an elderly priest that you need only four words to pray: "Thank you" and "Help me".

Sometimes I start, therefore, by thanking God – or the universe or whoever I feel like praying to – for anything that I appreciate in my life. This is a bit like keeping a blessings journal. When I'm feeling really lonely, I can't think of anything to write in my blessings journal and I can't think of anything to thank God for either. I don't feel much gratitude for anything. Sometimes I just have to start small. Even with something as small as a mug of hot tea. Then I ask God for help.

However, my most meaningful prayers go beyond words. I stop trying to talk to God as if he's a person sitting

167

next to me and I start just delving into my feelings. If I'm having a good day and feeling content, I just try to enjoy my feelings, to share them with God. If I'm feeling fed up and lonely, I try to go deeper into those feelings, to sit with them, rather than trying to push them away and ignore them. There's a saying "A problem shared is a problem halved." Sometimes when I share my feelings like this with God, they seem to diminish. It's hard to explain but I feel better afterwards.

A book that's really helped me is *Growing Into Silence* by Paul Nicholson. It was written to accompany the BBC2 programme *The Big Silence*, which was what first inspired me to go on a silent retreat (I'll describe that in Idea 41). Paul Nicholson advises that you can begin simply by being aware of each individual part of your body, starting with your toes and working upwards, flexing and relaxing each muscle in turn and allowing your point of awareness to eventually rest in the centre of yourself. Or you can simply focus on the breath, a technique also suggested by Zen teacher and writer, Cheri Huber. I've found that both of these techniques work for me, somehow allowing me to reach a "higher plane".

It doesn't really matter where I pray. It just has to feel safe and quiet. I usually like my bedroom best. "A friend always prays on the seashore," says Mark Bartlett in *Crossing*. "Another friend has a 'safe place' she goes to in the woods when times are difficult....A third person I know loves to walk the city streets, finding that the combination of company and aloneness that the street provides is perfect for prayer, while the people and buildings she passes evoke every conceivable human strength and weakness – every glory and every frailty."

A Buddhist monk once told me how he meditates and it seemed to be very similar to the way I pray. In his tradition, the normal method of meditation is to focus the attention entirely on the breath. But sometimes, feelings or cravings take your attention away, demanding attention and distracting from the meditation. For example, if someone is

168

an alcoholic, he told me, their craving for alcohol might be particularly strong and this might make focusing on their breath extremely difficult. Rather than trying to push the craving away, the monk said that you should allow yourself to feel the craving, to ride it like the crest of a wave. Eventually, the feeling would subside. This is different from trying to distract yourself from a craving or an unpleasant feeling, which I normally attempt by having a bag of crisps, a glass of wine or by putting the TV on.

If I'm honest, I'm not 100% sure of the difference between prayer and meditation. Elizabeth Gilbert writes in *Eat Pray Love* that "There's a difference between meditation and prayer, though both practices seek communication with the divine. I've heard it said that prayer is the act of talking to God, while meditation is the act of listening."

What I am hoping for, when I get down on my knees, is a *conversation* with God, a balance of listening and talking, of meditating and praying, because it's surely through conversation, through a two-way dialogue, that I will find the connection that I'm seeking.

"Prayer goes far beyond merely asking for benefits for oneself or for others," says psychiatrist Anthony Storr in his well-known book *Solitude*. "Prayer can be a public act of worship; but the person who prays in private feels himself to be alone in the presence of God. This is another way of putting the individual in touch with his deepest feelings. In some religions, no response to prayer from any supernatural being is even expected. Prayer is undertaken, not with the intention of influencing a deity, nor with any hope of prayers being directly answered, but in order to produce a harmonious state of mind. Prayer and meditation facilitate integration by allowing time for previously unrelated thoughts and feelings to interact."

Idea 41: Learn to enjoy silence

Removing oneself voluntarily from one's habitual environment promotes self-understanding and contact with those inner depths of being which elude one in the hurly-burly of day-to-day life.
~ Anthony Storr, *Solitude*

One of the things I used to hate most about being alone was the silence. When I first lived alone, I'd rush in and put the TV on, volume blaring, before even taking off my coat and boots. At least with the sound of a soap opera in the background, I could pretend that I had companionship.

Then one day I watched the programme *The Big Silence* on BBC2. Five normal people were plucked from their everyday lives and sent to stay in a Jesuit retreat centre in North Wales. I'd been on retreat a few times by this stage. But they weren't silent retreats. They were the sorts of retreats where you sit around with other people and enjoy thought-provoking conversations. The thought of a silent retreat…and for 8 whole days….well, I just couldn't contemplate it.

The participants in the programme seemed to find it difficult too. They moaned about the food and the lack of hot water. They cheated, having sneaky cigarettes and whispered conversations outside the gates of the centre. There was almost a mutiny as one person tried to cajole the others into going to the local pub. Only one of the participants was a practising Christian – the others were either lapsed or didn't believe in God at all. One man, Jon, seemed to hate the experience from the start. In the silent nights at the retreat centre, he recorded his video diary, speaking of his deep loneliness.

But by episode 3, something was different. Jon seemed to be a changed man. He seemed to have made some kind of deep spiritual connection with God. His loneliness seemed to have gone too: it seemed to have been replaced with a purpose and he talked of swapping his entrepreneurial life-style running a couple of profitable companies for a career that would benefit other people: psychotherapy. The change seemed miraculous and I decided that I wanted that experience for myself. The day after I watched that third and final episode, I emailed the retreat centre and booked myself on the same 8 day silent retreat.

As the retreat grew nearer, I felt more anxious. But, I reasoned, this was an ordeal that I was putting myself through in order to feel stronger at the other end. I reckoned that by facing up to my loneliness, far away from the security blankets of home, friends and television, I would finally realise that it wasn't such a frightening thing after all. I wanted to stare my loneliness down if you like, to deliberately put myself in a position where I knew I would be lonely – and bored – and see if I could finally make it go away. It didn't quite work out like that.

On the first afternoon when I got there, I made myself a little timetable, filling in meal times, mass times, and the hour that I'd have each day to talk with my spiritual adviser (that's the only time when you're officially allowed to speak). I worked out what time I'd go to bed and get up then calculated how much time I'd have to fill in and what I could do with that time: read the Bible (that was the only book you were officially supposed to read), write, walk, go running or use the well-stocked art room to get creative.

But the problem with that strategy was that it was how I normally lived. I spent my days following lists and timetables, ticking things off my "to do" list all day every day, even at the weekends. That strategy wasn't really working in my everyday life. I knew I needed to do something different. So early on in the retreat, I abandoned the timetable and started doing what I *felt* like doing. So if I wanted to go for a walk, I went for a walk. If I wanted to sit and drink tea and eat Jaffa cakes and write in my journal, that's what I did. An awful lot of Jaffa cakes were consumed in the course of that retreat. Instead of worrying about

171

whether I should be sitting around eating Jaffa cakes, whether I was being productive enough, whether I was achieving anything, I just asked myself the question, "Am I enjoying this? Is this what I want to be doing?"

The silence allowed me to form a deeper connection with my inner most self, with that deep authentic "real me" who often stays buried in a world of habits and social obligations and work commitments. It allowed me to form a deeper connection with that "other" which I call God. But strangely enough, it also allowed me to form some deep and long-lasting connections with some of the other participants on the retreat. OK, so a bit of cheating did go on. We did have the occasional conversation. But most of the time, we formed connections in the silence. The closest friend I met there was a woman who was about my age. We went walking together most days, usually in complete silence and we formed a deep friendship that has continued long after we left the retreat centre. We're still friends now.

On the last morning, we got up at dawn and went walking up the hill behind the retreat centre. We tried to take pictures of ourselves together, holding the camera with outstretched arms. We just couldn't manage to get a good shot – we kept getting the top of our heads silhouetted against the beautiful sunrise across the Colwyn Bay. This made us laugh till we cried. It's strange how you can have a good laugh without even speaking to someone.

The whole week was full of laughter in fact – so far from the ordeal that I thought it would be. Little things seemed to bring so much joy and fun. This might be a case of "you really had to be there" but spotting a Henry vacuum cleaner being wheeled through the dining room by one of the cleaning staff had me in fits of giggles. The vacuum cleaner seemed to have such a smug smile on his face, as if he was saying, "Ha! I'm allowed to make a noise and you're not!" My own personal favourite was that my friend had requested a gluten free, sugar free diet as that's what she has at home. The kitchen had dutifully obliged and she was given special meals all week. But every evening, the pair of us would guiltily devour whole packets of Jaffa cakes, all that deep thought and fresh air having made us really hungry.

The whole experience of 8 days in silence was extremely powerful. It promoted a kind of deep connection. Was the silence something that put me in touch with God or was it something that put me in touch with my inner self? Either way, the experience was life-changing. At least, I felt like I had been fundamentally changed. If you think of an earthquake: massive plates under the ground move causing the landscape of the world on the surface to completely change. I felt like something massive had shifted within me and that, as a result, my ordinary life had completely changed. They weren't just surface changes in other words – like going on a diet or having a new haircut would change your appearance. These changes ran deep.

Going on retreat kick-started my experiments with silence, but looking back, I could probably have learnt to be more comfortable with silence by simply being silent at home. Since the retreat, I've been incorporating short periods of silence into my daily life. I don't mean just being silent whilst I'm doing the washing up, but having periods of sitting still and being silent, taking time to reflect on things. It gives me time to really feel my feelings, if that makes sense, instead of brushing them aside. "Just being still, staying through it, being present," says writer Helena Wilkinson in *Breaking Free from Loneliness*, "creates a fire, an energy that literally burns away our desire to continue our old patterns."

Continuing with those periods of daily silence in my everyday life hasn't always been easy. Having to go to work can really get in the way. But I have tried to be less busy and to pray and meditate more. I don't watch nearly as much TV and not because I'm on some kind of "I mustn't watch so much TV because psychologists say it's bad for me" way, but simply because I don't *want* to. It isn't that I

173

am imposing some kind of Dickensian discipline on myself, in order to better myself. These days, I simply enjoy silence.

Idea 42: Participate in organised religion

The soul hardly ever realizes it, but whether he is a believer or not,
his loneliness is really a homesickness for God.
~ Hubert van Zeller

Studies have shown that people who follow a religion are happier than those who don't, but it isn't clear if this is down to the religion itself or the social network that goes with it. Perhaps participating in an organised religion makes us feel happier and less lonely because we feel a connection to God, or perhaps it's simply another way of connecting to other people.

"There is increasing evidence that religion and the inclination to form social networks are both part of our biological heritage and that the two may be related," suggest Nicholas Christakis and James Fowler, authors of *Connected: The Amazing Power of Social Networks and How They Shape Our Lives*. "Religion is one means of integrating people into a collective. A belief in God can have relevance to social networks in a direct way: God can actually be seen as part of the social network."

In other words, God becomes one of the "people" in the network. What's more, everyone in that network is connected to God and he (or she) cannot be removed. God can't suddenly decide that he's had enough of that particular group of friends and is going to hang out with someone else. This makes the social network, according to Christakis and Fowler, more stable.

I love the idea of "six degrees of separation" – everyone, it's suggested, is on average only six steps away from a connection with any other person on earth. There is even a game called "Six Degrees of Kevin Bacon" where the goal is to link any actor on the planet to Kevin Bacon through no more than six connections. Two actors are connected if they have appeared in a movie or commercial together.

If God is at the centre of a social network and everyone in that network is connected to him, then there is *never* more than one degree of separation between one person in the network and another person,. Apparently, this makes the network very stable indeed. "People who felt a connection to God," say Christakis and Fowler, "would have a way of feeling connected to others, because through God everyone is a 'friend of a friend.'"

When psychologist Catalin Mamali asked people to draw "maps" to show people to whom they felt close and to draw the interconnections on those maps, a significant number of people included God on their map and connected him (or her) to everyone else.

But could this really work in practice? Could having God as a person on my social map and participating in organised religion with other people who also have him on *their* social maps really make me feel less lonely?

I've had various experiences with organised religion over the years. My initial experience was as a child at a very evangelical school. The ideas taught to us at school did not really fit in with my ideas about God so often I felt excluded, as if I was doing something "wrong" in terms of my religious beliefs. This made me feel lonely. As an adult, marrying – and then divorcing – an ordained Church of England priest did not make me feel any more at ease with organised religion.

But I still felt that there was something out there other than just us, some kind of divine, creative energy and I chose to call that energy God. I also felt the need to connect with other people who shared that belief.

Eventually, I ventured into a Meeting House of the Religious Society of Friends or Quakers, as they're more commonly known. I was attracted by the Quakers partly because I had met one or two Quakers who seemed so at peace with the world and their place within it and partly because of its lack of dogma. There was nothing that I had

176

to sign up to believing. There were people at the weekly meetings who were committed Christians, others who were atheists and others who talked of the "Light" because they didn't like the word God. The Quakers were committed to believing in peace and looking after the planet and seeing everyone as equal. People of any religion and any sexuality were welcome at meetings. *Everyone* was made very welcome at meetings. It's daunting walking into a new place for the first time, but from the word go, I felt like I was part of something, I felt a strong sense of connection and belonging.

Eventually, I decided to brave going to church. I tried several churches. One had very dogmatic views so didn't suit me. At another, no-one bothered to speak to me, and I slipped out of the service at the end without staying for a cup of tea. I'd felt so unwelcome. Finally, I plucked up courage to walk up the steps of another local church. I have never had such a warm welcome anywhere.

Taking part in organised religion works for me. Usually. One Christian leader said to me that no-one should ever feel lonely because God is always with us and we are never alone. Even if we have no *human* friends, she said, Jesus is our friend and he is always there for us. That approach just *doesn't* help me: if anything, it makes me feel like a failed Christian. I felt a sense of relief when I read these words written by the Benedictine monk Mark Bartlett in his book, *Crossing*: "God is no use in bed. God does not hold you when you are down. He does not take you clubbing, to the cinema, or cook you a meal. He doesn't smell good or feel warm beside you."

God is great to talk to and I get much comfort from my belief in God, but I also want someone to hold me when I'm down, cook me a meal and take me to the cinema, though I'm not bothered about the clubbing. Going to church has become an important and meaningful ritual in my life, but I've realised that I need that connection to God *in addition to*, not *instead of, a* connection to other human beings.

177

In 2000, a study by Le Roux found that praying, attending church and having faith in Jesus were all shown to be negative predictors of loneliness. There's also research that suggests that those who value collectivism over individualism are less likely to be lonely. This might explain why those who are actively involved in a church are less likely to feel lonely, since the church places an emphasis on community and collectivism.

Previous research in 1985 had pointed to a similar negative correlation between loneliness and spiritual well-being. 64 chronically ill people and 64 randomly chosen healthy adults participated in the study. Their degree of both loneliness and spiritual well-being were measured. In both groups, according to Arthur E. Dell Orto and Paul W. Power in their book *Psychological and Social Impact of Illness and Disability*, there was an inverse correlation between loneliness and spiritual well-being.

Whilst these studies show that you are less likely to be lonely if you are religious, finding God is not a miracle cure for your loneliness, though there are plenty of people giving advice on the internet who would seem to suggest that it is. Not everyone is religiously inclined and I think that going to a church service if I didn't believe there was any truth in what was being preached would probably make me more, rather than less lonely, because I'd feel like the "odd one out".

In the words of Emily White, author of *Lonely: A Memoir*: "I think that one thing a religious service does is allow you to see other people as 'safe.' Loneliness cues threat perceptions, making us see the people around us as potential hazards. And everything—at least in the church I went to—was so hushed, the people so respectful and deferential, the lighting so soft, that it let me break out of the pattern of feeling threatened around others. It let me be with others while feeling (at least for the duration of the service) secure. I think this is an extremely important element in overcoming loneliness, and one that should be more widely available."

178

PART 5:
ESTABLISH A
CONNECTION WITH
NATURE

Idea 43: Grow a plant

Gardening is cheaper than therapy and you get tomatoes.
~ Author Unknown

Yet again, I'm going to mention the television programme *Making Slough Happy*. During the programme, the residents of Slough were encouraged to grow plants in order to make them feel happier. One of the "happiness scientists" roamed the streets of Slough offering free bedding plants and packets of seeds to passers-by. Not many were keen to take him up on his offer, but actually, the therapeutic properties of gardening are widely recognised. In 2011, the NHS hit the headlines in the UK with news that they were trying out a new treatment for stressed and depressed patients: an 8 week gardening course. A £3000 NHS Health and Wellbeing grant was used to fund this course as a trial in Southampton. The aim was to offer a natural solution to the issues of depression, anxiety and low self-esteem.

I never imagined, when I lived in a flat in London, that I would enjoy gardening. It was something my dad did! But then I moved to a house in the countryside, with a garden. One of the first things I did, once I'd bought a new sofa and painted the lounge, was to dig up the lawn and replace it with gravel so that I didn't have to bother doing any gardening. It just didn't appeal.

Then the spring came, and I thought I'd brighten my gravelled area with a few pots of plants so that I could sit out and enjoy the sunshine. Next I thought I'd make my own hanging baskets and pretty soon, I was moving to a house with a bigger garden – and no gravel – because I fancied giving gardening a try. It's addictive. It really boosts my mood. For one thing, it gets me out in the fresh air and daylight. It's good exercise too, thereby boosting the endorphin levels.

I'm not sure *why* gardening is so fantastic. It's still a mystery to me why I like it so much when I thought I'd hate it. Apparently, gardening is a popular activity in prisons and lower levels of violent incidents are reported in prisons where gardening is offered as a regular activity. Nelson Mandela had a small garden whilst in prison on Robben Island. He wrote in his autobiography: "A garden is one of the few things in prison that one could control."

Perhaps that's the reason. When I'm feeling lonely, I don't feel that I'm in control of my life. Life simply hasn't gone the way I wanted it to go. I haven't met the right partner, found a job that makes me feel happy and secure, had a family or made enough friends. I start to feel hopeless, like I'm incapable of changing anything in my life and there's nothing that I can do to improve my own situation. Gardening allows me to take back that control: I decide what I plant where and watch my efforts reap results. Well, sometimes they reap results. Sometimes, nothing happens.

There's something magical about gardening. It seems like a chore in February, particularly in cold weather, to raise myself from the sofa and leave the warmth of the house to head out into the chilly back garden. Preparing the ground for the vegetables that I'll plant when the frosts have gone is such arduous work. Digging the hard soil can seem like too big a job. Clearing the weeds is back-breaking. Sometimes, even putting on my old clothes can feel like too much effort. But once I'm out there, I start to enjoy myself.

Gardening also helps me to connect with nature. Often a blackbird or a robin will hover around where I'm digging, hoping to grab an unlucky worm or two. It's thrilling to see the first shoots from seeds that I've planted poking their heads above the soil. It's even more thrilling to pull up potatoes that I've grown myself or eat peas fresh from their pods.

The natural cycle of preparing the soil, sowing the seeds, watering, weeding, tending the plants and finally harvesting the crops really connects me to the world around

181

me. That connection to the natural world is one that I used to underestimate: I thought that my loneliness could only be overcome by connecting to other people. Whilst feeling a sense of connection with nature isn't a substitute for relationships with other human beings, it can still bring great satisfaction and contentment, so it's been an important part of my journey out of loneliness.

Idea 44: Get into the open air

The best remedy for those who are afraid, lonely or unhappy is to go outside, somewhere where they can be quiet, alone with the heavens, nature and God. Because only then does one feel that all is as it should be.
~ Anne Frank

"It's vitally important that we get into nature as much as we can," said psychologist Dr. Richard Stevens in that programme I keep mentioning, as he headed off into the countryside for a camping trip with some of the participants.

One of the people whose words most touched me when I saw the programme for the first time was Ruth LeGoff. Ruth was an artist who, according to a newspaper article published at the time of the series, "had been suffering for seven or eight years with mental health problems, chronic depression and anxiety, and thought she should give the programme a go." There was just something about Ruth that I liked: she was so honest about her feelings and I could really relate to what she said.

As Ruth sat with the rest of the group around the campfire on the first evening, the conversation flowed and people said they already felt a real sense of community with each other, even though they'd only just met. "Most of our evolutionary history has been sitting around fires like this," observed Dr. Richard Stevens. "I think one of the problems of everyday life is living in housing estates, and that feeling of alienation".

Ruth lived on a housing estate. She'd been there three months and said that she hadn't even met her neighbours yet. On the camping trip, as she sat alone on a jetty looking across a beautiful lake, Ruth said that she wished she could stay longer, much longer.

183

We weren't meant to live in huge cities and concrete jungles, we were meant to live in places like this. I think when you're sort of in your twenties or early thirties, you kind of look for happiness in odd places and for me, pubs and clubs and stuff are an odd place to look for happiness. I've never found it and I remember being a teenager going to discos and I found they were the loneliest places on earth, they really were. I'd feel less lonely if I was on my own here than in the middle of a nightclub. There's just something about nature that is very soothing, very calming.

I liked Ruth's words because I've had a similar experience. As a teenager and a university student, I felt lonely at parties, discos and in nightclubs but I thought I *should* enjoy them. I thought I was the only one who didn't, and that's a very isolating feeling. As usual, hearing someone else express similar feelings to mine was such a relief.

But I wasn't too sure that I'd find being alone in the countryside any less lonely than going to a nightclub. I was wrong.

On my first silent retreat, which I described in Idea 41, I expected to feel great loneliness. In fact, that was one of my main motivations for going on the retreat in the first place. I wanted to face up to one of my biggest fears: my loneliness. During the retreat, to pass the time, I went on long country walks all alone, which is something I've never done before. I'm so used to going on group rambles or going out walking with friends. I'm used to having conversation as I walk along. I'm not used to walking for miles and miles in silence. But I thought I'd give it a go.

To my surprise, I wasn't lonely. I actually enjoyed the walks. I noticed things I wouldn't have noticed before, if I'd been busy chatting with someone. I felt at one with my environment, connected somehow. I enjoyed sunrises on my early morning walks and sunsets on later ones. I enjoyed birdsong and the sound of the wind rustling through the trees. I enjoyed changes in the weather. It sounds a bit grand to say that I felt part of a bigger picture, part of the whole of creation, but I did. I felt connected to everything around me. But can feeling a connection to the natural world really make me feel less lonely?

The social psychologist Erich Fromm wrote of the "contradiction inherent in human existence". Man stands apart from nature due to his awareness of himself and of his own mortality. As human beings, we are aware of life itself in a way that animals are not. This separates us from the rest of the natural world. And yet we are dependent *on* that natural world.

"Man," says Fromm in his book *The Heart of Man*, "is confronted with the frightening conflict of being a prisoner of nature, yet being free in his thoughts; being part of nature, and yet to be as it were a freak of nature; being neither here nor there. Human self-awareness has made man a stranger in the world, separate, lonely, and frightened."

It was Erich Fromm who first used the term "biophilia" which literally means "love of life or living systems." The American biologist, E.O. Wilson also uses the term in the same sense when he suggests that biophilia describes "the connections that human beings subconsciously seek with the rest of life."

Emily White writes in *Lonely: A Memoir*, "E.O. Wilson... has described ours as the 'Age of Loneliness.' He's not speaking metaphorically. He means that, as we continue to let species perish, we're inevitably going to feel more isolated and bereft in the world they've left behind. With loneliness conceptualized in this reasonable way - as a state that reflects, at least in part, our ties to the world around us - it's impossible to think that the extinction rate can climb upward while the loneliness rate remains unchanged. Environmental losses will translate into personally felt absences... extinction is a gradual, perpetual, and silent good-bye."

185

The biophilia hypothesis suggests that there is a connection between human beings and other living systems. Perhaps that explains why I feel less lonely when I take active steps to deepen the connection that I feel with the natural world around me.

Thomas Berry, the cultural historian, believed that we need to see the universe as "subjects to be communed with, not objects to be explained." In his essay *Loneliness and Presence*, Berry relates the story of the treaty negotiations in the mid 19th century between the white European settlers and the Suquamish, a Native American Tribe on the North Pacific coast. The head of the Suquamish, Chief Seattle, writes Berry, "is reported to have said that when the last animals will have perished 'humans would die of loneliness'. This was an insight that might never have occurred to a European settler."

"Yet this need for more-than-human companionship," Berry continues, "has significance and an urgency that we begin to appreciate in more recent times. To understand this primordial need that humans have for the natural world and its inhabitants we need only reflect on the needs of our children, the two-, three- and four-year-olds especially. We can hardly communicate with them in any meaningful way except through pictures and stories of humans and animals and fields and trees, of flowers, birds and butterflies, of sea and sky. The child experiences the 'friendship relation' that exists among all things throughout the universe...Indeed we cannot be truly ourselves in any adequate manner without all our companion beings throughout the earth. This larger community constitutes our greatest self."

Idea 45: Find furry and feathered friends

The difference between friends and pets is that friends we allow into our company, pets we allow into our solitude.
~ Robert Brault

I mentioned earlier that doing things that I enjoyed as a child can be a great source of fun, and sometimes comfort. During my childhood, I kept scrapbooks, did lots of writing and watched endless ballet videos. Another thing I enjoyed as a child was feeding the ducks. When I was about five, the Wildfowl and Wetlands Trust opened a new centre just a couple of miles from my house. My parents signed us up as members and we began making regular excursions to feed the ducks. 37 years later, I am *still* a member. Feeding the ducks, the birds in my garden or even just stopping to pat a horse when I'm out walking doesn't completely get rid of my feelings of loneliness, but it often makes me feel a little better. It's my DIY version of "animal assisted therapy".

The earliest documented case of "animal assisted therapy" took place at the York Retreat, led by William Tuke, an English Quaker, in the late 18th century. The grounds were full of small domestic animals that the patients could interact with.

Having a pet seems to have an effect on more than just morale: studies show that it might have physical benefits too. In 2002, Karen Allen of the State University of New York at Buffalo measured the stress levels and blood pressure in people while they contended with performing 5 minutes of mental maths or holding a hand in ice water. Half of the people tested were pet-owners. Some participants did the tasks on their own, and others with a spouse, a close friend or with their pet.

The people who did the test with their pet had smaller spikes in blood pressure and their heart-rates returned more quickly to baseline. They also made fewer numerical errors. If only I'd been allowed to take Brecon, our old pet Labrador, into my Maths 'A' Level exam.

In a second study, Allen put half of a group of stockbrokers suffering from high-blood pressure onto drugs and told the other half of them to get a pet. Six months later, the pet owners were found to have significantly lower blood pressure than those who had been taking the drugs.

Since research indicates a possible link between loneliness and high blood pressure, getting a pet might be a way of off-setting the high blood pressure that loneliness has been shown to cause *and* reducing the emotional suffering of loneliness at the same time.

In fact, studies have shown that animal assisted therapy consistently lowers loneliness scores. Some experts have argued that this is because the person receiving a visit from an animal, in a hospital or nursing home for example, also gets the chance to interact with that animal's handler. But in the United States, there was a study of 37 nursing home residents, all of whom scored high on a loneliness scale. In the study, all the participants received a visit from a dog. Some of them got to spend time alone with the dog, whilst others spent time with a dog *and* other people. After the visits, they were assessed again on the loneliness scale and those who'd spent time on their own with the dog were found to feel less lonely than those who had spent time with the dog and other people.

"It was a strange finding," said William A. Banks, M.D., professor of geriatrics at Saint Louis University School of Medicine. "We expected the group dog visits were going to work better, but they didn't. The residents found a little quiet time with the pooch is a lot nicer than spending time with a dog and other people."

"Pets do wonders for our physical and mental well-being," says Liz Hoggard, author of *How to Be Happy*. "They provide their owners with unconditional love and loyalty and in return, we experience the pleasure of caring for an animal, feel needed and enjoy the opportunities it provides for play and amusement …Relationships with animals are largely free of the psychological games inherent in human relationships," Liz continues. "Pets allow us to have 'risk-free' relationships…Pets are a form of social capital. They help us to develop empathy and broaden our focus beyond ourselves, making us feel connected to a larger world."

There is perhaps another reason why having a dog might make us feel connected to a larger world. I often go walking with one of my closest friends in the park and along the canal near her home. Recently, she's got a dog, and suddenly, other people are stopping to chat to us: they stop initially to pat the dog and this develops into a conversation. Remember Leil Lowndes' advice to get a Whatzit so people would find it easy to strike up conversations with you? Well, perhaps dogs are living, breathing Whatzits!

Perhaps the old cliché that a dog is man's best friend might actually be true. Personally, I choose not to have a pet: they're expensive, time-consuming and I don't want to have to go out walking two or three times a day, come rain or shine. But if, like me, you want contact with animals *without* actually getting a pet, there are plenty of alternatives that are well worth exploring: dog walking for the local pet rescue centre, horse riding lessons or simply feeding the ducks.

PART 6:
FURTHER
SUGGESTIONS

Idea 46: Give yourself a daily treat

*God gave us the gift of life; it is up to us to give ourselves
the gift of living well.*
~ Voltaire

This is positively the last time I'll mention *Making Slough Happy,* but here's one last tip from the programme: "Give yourself a treat every day and take the time to really enjoy it."

"Everyone would benefit from a daily treat," say Gillian Butler and Tony Hope, authors of *Managing Your Mind: The Mental Fitness Guide.* "Small pleasures make life easier and more pleasurable. But make sure that you do not use treats that fail to satisfy. If rewards like shopping, or having another cigarette, drink or doughnut only perpetuate the search for pleasure, or make you feel better or less lonely only briefly, they may be the wrong kinds of treats for you."

I have, on occasion, reached for the wrong kind of treat: in my case, a glass of wine. For me, it's all easy for a glass to become a bottle of wine and I could easily find myself far too dependent on alcohol as a way out of feeling lonely. One of my friends has been a recovering alcoholic for nearly two decades. He once said to me, "Jenny, it started off because I was looking for love in a glass." For me cakes and chocolate biscuits would carry a similar risk factor. Before long, I'm comfort-eating and putting on weight and my self-esteem sinks that little bit lower.

My favourite sorts of treats, the ones that really work on my loneliness, are things that I can *do.* I try to cook myself a fantastic meal from scratch, if I want to use food as a treat, rather than just buying something ready-made. The satisfaction level is much higher and I'm not only giving myself something nice to eat, I am *doing* something nice for myself, the way a friend or a lover would. Plus the creative act of making something brings a satisfaction all of its own.

I'm not really into retail therapy but I like the occasional splurge. Again, I try to buy something that I'll enjoy doing rather than a dress that I look good in but will never get the opportunity to wear. So I'll get a book that I've wanted to read for ages, the DVD of a film that I've always wanted to see or something from Hobbycraft. Those beautiful blank notebooks from Paperchase are one of my favourite treats, along with coloured gel pens so I can get creative and start journaling. I've also treated myself to theatre tickets – though I'm not 100% convinced that I really enjoy going on my own - or I simply listen to one of my favourite pieces of music.

Often, when I'm reading about loneliness, there's a focus on our emotional needs, but our physical needs are forgotten. Touch is something that I've often missed in those lonely times in my life. I miss simply having someone give me a hug. Psychologist Richard Stevens, head of the team of experts on *Making Slough Happy*, believes that we don't make enough physical contact with each other in British culture. "Touch is the basic language of love," he says. "A child in distress is calmed by being held tight in a parent's arms. Most adults need caresses and cuddles too."

According to Rae Andre, author of *Positive Solitude,* "No definitive research has been done that will give us guidelines as to how much human touch we each need. Probably, as in most things, the range of human need differs." If you're missing being touched, suggests Andre, "Make love to yourself. You are the person who knows how to touch you best."

Another option might be to get a massage. I have tried it and I can't honestly say that it affected my feelings of loneliness one way or the other but I know people who swear by it. One of my friends is a fully qualified masseuse and, when she heard I was writing a book about loneliness, she told me that many of her clients are lonely and come to her for a little TLC.

193

One thing that I do enjoy is acupuncture. My doctor suggested trying it when I was going through a period of having very persistent migraines. I'm not sure how effective the acupuncture was at getting rid of the migraines, but I began to really look forward to the in-depth conversations each week. The acupuncture sessions offered me the chance to talk and feel really listened to.

"Massage and acupuncture sessions," says Carl Honoré, in *In Praise of Slow*, "usually last an hour during which the practitioner talks to and touches the patient. It may sound trite but in a world where everyone is constantly dashing around and real connections between people are few and far between, a little tender loving care goes a long way."

Idea 47: Find what you're missing

The trouble is not that I am single and likely to stay single,
but that I am lonely and likely to stay lonely.
~ Charlotte Brontë

Not all loneliness is the same. Some of us feel lonely because our circumstances have changed – we've moved to a new city, we've changed jobs and miss our friends in our old workplace, we've been bereaved or got divorced or our best friend has emigrated. The experts call this "situational loneliness" – when circumstances become more favourable again, the loneliness disappears. Some people have an active social life and a family around them but still feel lonely. Their loneliness is more long-term and is termed "chronic loneliness".

Another popular way of categorizing loneliness was developed by the American sociologist, Robert S. Weiss. Weiss identified two types of loneliness: emotional loneliness and social loneliness.

Emotional loneliness is connected to attachment theory: when children are separated from their parents, they experience separation distress. I remember this all too well as a child the first time my mother left me, aged 3, to go to an evening class. I banged the back door for hours, desperate for her to come back. (Just so my mother isn't prosecuted, I'd like to add here that I wasn't left *alone*: my father was looking after me.) Years later, I encountered this separation distress on my very first day as a qualified teacher, when several of my 4 year old charges, attending school for the very first time, decided they didn't want *their* mums to leave them. There were floods of tears, howling and temper tantrums all round. And that was just the mothers. (I'm not kidding – the mothers *were* crying as much as the children.)

Understanding the different types of loneliness helps me understand *my* loneliness and why I suffer it, *when* I suffer it.

As adults, our attachment forms to our romantic partners and we suffer distress when we are separated from them. Weiss described emotional loneliness as "separation distress without an object." In other words, the person is suffering loneliness because they lack a romantic partner. I feel lonely because I haven't found Mr Right but I am already *attached* just to the idea of him, even though I haven't yet met him. It's not that I don't value my network of friends or the great relationship I have with my parents – I do. But I miss having the intimacy of a close, romantic relationship.

This idea of attachment explains why my loneliness is often at its worst when I've just met a potential partner. I've never understood this. I've always thought, "I've just met someone nice, I should be feeling great, not lonely!" but the fact is that I sometimes become too quickly attached to the idea of this new man being a more permanent fixture in my life and impatient for it to happen and then when I don't see him as often as I'd like, I begin to feel lonely.

I used to think that everyone's loneliness was the same, but my friends seem to feel loneliness at different times to me. Social loneliness is what people feel when they lack a wider social network. This is the type of loneliness felt by housewives who have good marriages but still feel lonely. It's the loneliness of relying too much on your romantic relationship to provide your sense of connection to other people. Someone who feels this might say that they've not got enough close friends or that they don't feel part of an extended family. I am not part of a big, extended family but I don't feel lonely because of that. Yet one of my friends does. She has a very good marriage to a very lovely man and a lot of close friends, but she has a deep-seated longing to be part of a big extended family.

Different types of relationship fulfil different needs in our lives so most people need both a good network of friends *and* a romantic relationship in order to avoid feeling lonely. Pin-pointing exactly what I felt I was missing when I felt lonely meant I could take pro-active steps towards finding it.

Initially, when I was trying to "cure" my feelings of loneliness, and didn't really understand where they were coming from, I tried to get out more. I actively sought more social opportunities and I tried to find more friends. I was successful in this: I had a busy diary and was hardly ever at home. My list of friends grew and grew. But I *still* felt lonely, and it was hard to fathom out why. Why did I still feel lonely when I knew so many people? When I felt popular for the first time in my life? When I was having to turn down social invitations because I was already double-booked? Why did I still feel lonely when I was almost never alone?

When I read Robert Weiss' theory, it suddenly made sense. I was missing the closeness of a romantic relationship and having lots of friends and an active social life weren't a substitute for that because they fulfilled a *different* need in my life.

So rather than devoting quite so much attention to my social life, if I was to find freedom from loneliness, I needed to devote more time to finding a romantic partner. I'm not saying that I should spend *all* my time going to singles nights and speed-dating or sitting at home browsing profiles on internet dating. But, I needed to stop going out for girly dinners *every* evening with my female friends to places where there were absolutely no opportunities to meet men. I needed to make sure that I put myself in places where that lucky encounter with the right man actually *has* a chance of happening. As my housemate once said, "You are not going to meet Mr Right sitting on the sofa of number 87!" – in other words, in our house.

Someone whose problem is not emotional loneliness, but social loneliness, would need to do the opposite to me: they'd need to find opportunities to meet people *other* than their romantic partner.

197

Having a sense of "not fitting in" was another thing that I identified as causing my feelings of loneliness. So I had to find places where I did feel that I fitted in. The problem with the active social life that I'd initially pursued in order to help me find freedom from loneliness was that it often involved going to places where I didn't really fit in: a very drunken weekend in Centre Parcs, for example, with a group of people who were lovely but who really liked to party, when I wanted to be in bed at half past ten with a good book. I simply stopped doing those things, focusing instead on going to places where I do feel I can fit in, like retreats, art classes or simply visiting my closest friends.

One of the worst things about loneliness is that feeling that it's happening *to* me, that it's beyond my control. Perhaps I will never find that elusive Mr Right – he's managed to evade me so far for a whole 42 years – but at least I feel that I am doing something, that I am being pro-active. Working out what I was missing and taking steps to find it put me back in control of my own life.

Idea 48: Get away from it all

All God's children need travelling shoes.
~ Maya Angelou

Getting away from the routine of daily life and changing my environment can be a fantastic way to make things seem better. I love travelling. The more far-flung the better. I love seeing other cultures. I love warmer climates, tropical rainforests, exotic cocktails, great historical sights. I love the adventure of going somewhere new and seeing something different.

I've been lucky enough to visit Australia, South America, South East Asia, Africa and several countries in Europe. I haven't stayed in luxury hotels – mostly I've been backpacking – but I've seen the beautiful temples of Angkor Wat, admired the views from Macchu Pichu and scuba-dived on the Great Barrier Reef. I've photographed lion cubs in Tanzania, orang-utans in Borneo and hippos in Uganda. I've even swum with piranhas in the Amazon.

When I got divorced, I missed having someone to holiday with. I went away with friends a few times, but gradually, people found partners of their own and settled down and my pool of potential travelling companions shrunk and shrunk. I didn't really have anyone to go away with. I wanted to go away on my own but I was nervous and fearful of being lonely. Would I enjoy a holiday without a travelling companion, without someone to turn to and say, "Isn't that a beautiful sunset?" Who would I eat dinner with? Would I be safe travelling in different cultures as a single woman?

The feelings of exhilaration and delight at being in a different country seem to disappear when I go travelling alone. I'm sure there are loads of people who love holidaying alone but it hasn't come naturally to me.

Having no travelling companion brings back all the feelings of loneliness that I've fought so hard to overcome. Being on my own, away from the safety of my home, makes my loneliness levels soar. These days, when I'm at home, my routines and hobbies and friendships all work together and I hardly ever feel lonely. But put me on a plane or a train, and take me somewhere new, and I feel like I am back to square one.

The writer Sark says she loves travelling alone because "the sense of adventure is very clear; all my tastes and preferences are honoured; meeting 'strangers'; sipping tea for hours; no destinations but my own; the sense that anything could happen. The challenging parts to travelling alone are: being scared; feeling all alone; relying only on yourself; not meeting anyone." But she points out, she can feel scared, alone and not meet anyone just as easily when she's at home as when she's travelling – so she might as well travel.

I feel much the same. Despite the loneliness and anxiety that accompany getting away for a week or two on my own, I still like travelling. I still feel better after a change of scene. I don't see want to miss out on getting a bit of summer sunshine in a warmer climate or seeing the Pyramids at Giza or drinking cappuccinos in a Venetian square simply because I don't have a travelling companion.

I've tried various different solutions to the problem of having no-one to travel with but still wanting to travel. The first idea was to go on holiday with a company that was popular amongst single travellers. There are a few of these around – I've been with Exodus and Explore and thoroughly enjoyed myself. These aren't singles holidays as such. The aim of the holiday is to see the sights or do some specific activity like walking or cycling, *not* to meet a partner (though some people do – one of my friends met her fiancé on an Explore holiday!)

Not everyone on my trips was on their own: on the holidays I've been on, the groups have always consisted of a mixture of couples and singles. But the fact that I wasn't the *only* person on my own made the holiday more enjoyable. I didn't feel like the odd one out.

Another thing I've tried is volunteering. I worked in a children's home in Tanzania for a week. It meant I had something to do during the day – and something useful too – and during the evening, I found there were lots of opportunities to socialise with the other volunteers. I later went to Uganda, where I'd volunteered to make a film to help the charity Five Talents with publicity. I had a great time and made good friends as a result.

Recently, my favourite type of "getting away from it all" has been going on retreat. I've already mentioned the silent retreat that I went on, but the first retreats I tried weren't silent at all. They weren't silent but it was still a long way from going on holiday to somewhere with a pool, lots of alcohol and a buzzing nightlife. I wasn't sure that going to stay in a monastery in the English countryside would be my sort of thing. I thought it would be far too religious and ... well, boring.

But to my surprise, it wasn't. One of the best things about being on retreat is that it feels like a totally safe environment. You are sheltered and protected and somehow, those feelings of isolation and fear start to evaporate. This made sense given that one of the reasons why we humans have evolved to feel a sense of loneliness is that we're safer in groups. On retreat, I quickly discovered that I feel completely safe even when I'm completely alone. My loneliness disappears.

My first retreat was to Worth Abbey in Sussex. I only went because I'd seen it on TV (in the BBC series *The Monastery*) and I was curious to see what a monastery was like. I'd never spoken to a monk before and I couldn't imagine what caused men to choose a life of celibacy. I didn't understand how anyone could choose to live without a life partner. It was unthinkable. Didn't they get lonely?

So motivated by idle curiosity rather than any kind of religious faith, I arrived for a weekend at Worth. I didn't expect to enjoy myself, but to my surprise I did.

201

That all-important sense of forging connections with other human beings often seems so elusive in every day life. But on retreat, it was easy. In that safe environment, people were very ready and willing to share their deepest fears and desires. We'd never met each other before, yet there we were, exchanging confidences like old friends. We quickly moved away from the usual small-talk that you have when you meet new people and into conversations of a depth that I just hadn't expected. Somehow, these deep conversations allowed me to feel a strong sense of connection to people I'd only just met.

I've been on several retreats since – mostly Christian with the exception of the Buddhist mindfulness retreat that I've already mentioned – and my experience has been the same every time.

These three ways of getting away from it all really suit me and have definitely played a part in alleviating my loneliness. I no longer feel that I have to wait for Mr Right to come along before I so much as open a holiday brochure.

Idea 49: Have a hot bath

Sorrow can be alleviated by good sleep, a bath and a glass of wine.
~ St. Thomas Aquinas

One of the things I like least about being single is getting into a cold bed on a cold winter's night and having no-one to snuggle up to. No warm man to give me a cuddle. And that is one of the things that triggers my loneliness. I've berated myself for this over the years, telling myself that it was a silly thing to be bothered about, to get upset over. After all, lots of people are single and perfectly content. But lying in a cold bed ... well, it just makes me feel miserable.

I've tried hot water bottles and they're ok, but my real discovery has been an electric blanket. I love my electric blanket. It makes all the difference. Getting into bed on a cold winter's night is now a treat, not an ordeal. And those lonely feelings of lying there shivering, longing for some human warmth and company, have pretty much gone away. Who would have thought that such a simple thing as an electric blanket could ease my loneliness?

It seems there is a scientific basis for my accidental discovery. Psychologists have discovered that social isolation really does make people feel cold. Researchers at the University of Toronto found that people who were feeling left out said that a room was colder than those people who were feeling included. This might explain why, when I'm in the house alone, I put the heating thermostat on 19 degrees. When my housemate gets in, he switches it back down to 17 and I don't ever notice the difference.

In a second experiment, the researchers asked a group of 52 students to play a computer simulated ball game. In the game, the ball was passed to some people lots of times, making them feel included. Other people were left out. The participants were then asked to choose between a variety of foods including hot soup and coffee and cold

203

drinks. The people who'd been left feeling unpopular, because the ball hadn't been passed to them, were much more likely to choose the hot soup and coffee over the cold drinks.

In the journal *Psychological Science*, Dr Chen-Bo Zhong who led the research said: "We found that the experience of social exclusion literally feels cold. This may be why people use temperature-related metaphors to describe social inclusion and exclusion."

Perhaps in the same way that someone who has seasonal affective disorder (SAD) might be helped with light therapy, raising the temperature by getting an electric blanket or having a hot drink might help someone who is feeling lonely or socially isolated.

In another study, researchers at Yale University discovered that having a hot bath can compensate for social isolation. They questioned 51 undergraduates and discovered that those who felt lonelier also tended to bath and shower for longer, using warmer water.

A second study confirmed that physical warmth can affect people's sense of social warmth. The participants were deceived into thinking that they were taking part in a product test of a small therapeutic pack, which could be either warm or cold. They had to hold the pack in the palm of their hand. Those who held the cold pack subsequently reported feeling more lonely than those who held the warm pack.

The researchers went on to perform a similar test, asking the participants to recall a time when they'd felt socially excluded. Recalling this time of social exclusion made the participants desire company and comforting activities like shopping. But this effect disappeared if they were given the warm therapeutic pack to hold. The researchers concluded that "...warm physical experiences were found to significantly reduce the distress of social exclusion."

Perhaps this is why we describe someone as having "a warm smile" or giving us "the cold shoulder". We instinctively connect someone's sociability – or lack of it – with physical temperature.

I think I've always instinctively turned to things like a warm bath, a hot water bottle, a soft blanket to cuddle up into, a bowl of steaming soup or a mug of hot chocolate when I've been feeling down and lonely. I even sometimes use the heat-mask that is supposed to help migraines. All of these things bring me a real sense of comfort - I just never realized why before.

Idea 50: Split empty times into manageable chunks

The best thing about the future is that it comes one day at a time.
~ Abraham Lincoln

I remember one Friday night not long after I became a single woman. I arrived home from work at about 6 p.m. Normally, there'd have been after work drinks with colleagues on a Friday night but everyone else was tied up with other things. So I had nothing planned for that evening. I had nothing planned for Saturday. Nor Sunday. No-one had invited me anywhere. I hadn't booked anywhere to go or anything to do. One long, lonely weekend. As I put my bags down and locked the front door behind me, I knew it will be just me all weekend. If I was lucky, I might have a conversation with the cashier at the supermarket as I did my weekly shop, but that would be the only time I spoke to anyone all weekend till I went back to work on Monday morning.

Those empty hours terrify me. Those empty hours when loneliness' best buddy comes knocking at the door: boredom. And once boredom has arrived, I know loneliness won't be too far behind him. As soon as I start to feel bored, I inevitably start to feel lonely.

The weekend stretches before me like a big gaping hole. There are things I want to do – the car and the kitchen could do with a good clean and I could cook some meals for the freezer so I don't have to do so much cooking during the week. But I don't know if I have the motivation.

It's that long, empty stretch of time that I find difficult to cope with. I cannot seem to find it within myself to do anything at all. And then, I feel bad because I am doing nothing. I know that if I could raise the energy to do something I would feel better but I just can't. I think that people with depression get like this. I don't think I have depression but I am definitely not happy.

I repeatedly log onto internet dating, Facebook and Hotmail to see if anyone has contacted me. Nobody has. It feels like every other human being on the planet is busy having a great weekend apart from me.

I want something exciting to happen but it feels like it never does. I try watching *Come Dine with Me* on More4 but the sight of people socialising at dinner parties makes me feel worse. It will be a relief to get back to work on Monday, just to speak to another human being.

My "list of things to do whenever I feel bored" is a bit of a help but still….it's that long stretch of empty time. It's an obstacle I can't seem to get over. It's Friday night and Monday morning seems light years away.

If I have a large, difficult job to do, it makes sense to split that job into smaller, more manageable tasks. So that's what I try to do with that long, difficult weekend. In my mind, I split it into smaller, more manageable chunks of time: into mornings, afternoons and evenings. Or even into two hour or one hour chunks. Anything. Anything that I feel is manageable for me.

I can get through Friday evening. I have had lots of evenings in on my own. But there are three evenings, two afternoons and two mornings to fill up. I take my "list of things to do whenever I feel bored" and start to plan. I set goals. I can do two things off the bored list on Saturday morning. I could do the shopping mid-afternoon on Saturday, thus breaking up the day and I could break the day up on Sunday with a walk somewhere. I could watch a DVD on Friday evening, do some cooking for the freezer on Saturday evening and cook myself a nice dinner whilst I'm at it as a treat and perhaps write some letters and emails on Sunday night so that I feel that I'm at least communicating with someone.

If I tackle one section of the weekend at a time, it's somehow easier to get through. And that goes for other stretches of time too. Sometimes the Christmas and New Year period can seem interminably long when you're single (see Idea 18 on planning for the difficult times.) Breaking

207

that holiday period up into more manageable chunks of time and working how to spend each one can work then too.

Admittedly, there are times when loneliness can make life itself seem like one long, empty stretch of time. When I was unemployed, for example, I didn't even have the comfort of knowing that after an empty weekend, I'd be returning to work on a Monday morning. But even then, splitting my time up worked. I found regular activities that broke the week down into more manageable sections of time, making the periods of emptiness shorter and the lonely days feel a bit less lonely.

Idea 51: Identify situations that will make you lonely

Knowing others is intelligence; knowing yourself is true wisdom.
Mastering others is strength; mastering yourself is true power.
~ Lao-Tzu

I have a life-threatening allergy to nuts, aspirin and penicillin. Needless to say, I avoid all of those things. Certain situations trigger my loneliness. I am not quite as good at avoiding those situations as I am at avoiding nuts, aspirin and penicillin and, worse still, I haven't even worked out what all of those situations are.

In *Positive Solitude,* author Rae Andre suggests making an inventory of "the times when you are alone and feel bored, tired, hostile or excluded – in general, when you feel lonely." For me, those times definitely included things like Christmas and birthdays – in other words the times when I most miss having that special person in my life. That's why I try to plan specifically for those occasions.

But there are other times too, times that occur on a more frequent basis. As I did my inventory, I realised that late afternoon is, for me, a difficult time of day. In the mornings, I wake with a sense of purpose. Either I'm spending the day home alone and have something specific that I want to do or I'm going out to do a job or meeting a friend. If I've stayed at home, by late afternoon, I'm getting bored of my own company and the task in hand. Even if I've been out somewhere, I often arrive home late in the afternoon and don't know quite what I want to get started on doing. Obviously, I can't avoid late afternoons – I can't remove a few hours from the clock face – so there's no choice but to work out how to deal with those times, even if it's just making a simple plan: "When I go home, I will make a cup of tea, cut a slice of cake and sit on the sofa with a gripping novel for a whole hour of pleasurable reading."

209

I've discovered that moving to a new place triggers my loneliness. It seemed like a great idea, a few years ago, to return to London. I had been offered a promotion. I had already lived there before and liked it. I had lost touch with a lot of people but I still had a few friends there, and there were infinitely more opportunities for socialising and meeting new people than there seemed to be in Yorkshire. But it didn't work out like that: I missed my friends from my old job, my London friends were used to seeing me on occasional visits rather than incorporating me into their lives on a more regular basis, and getting the tube on my own all the way across town to go to all those social events made me feel lonelier than ever.

John Cacioppo, author of *Loneliness: Human Nature and the Need for Social Connection,* points out that knowing that we have are sensitive to loneliness or have an increased propensity to be lonely enables us to take avoidance action, to avoid those things that trigger our loneliness, in the same way that I avoid peanuts and penicillin to avoid triggering my allergies. So realising that moving house or changing jobs can cause me to feel lonely, I think twice these days about doing it. I'm not saying that I'll *never* move house or change job but I do give it more careful consideration.

As well as identifying those times that make me most lonely, because I try to be a positive person, I decided to identify those times when I'm *least* lonely. I realised that I almost never feel lonely in two situations: when I'm home alone and engaged in something purposeful that I really want to do; and when I'm with one of the half dozen people whom I consider to be my closest friends. Now I've realised that, I can plan my time accordingly.

Idea 52: Admit the problem

A problem shared is a problem halved.
~ Traditional proverb

I felt like a loser when I felt lonely. At school, I was *always* last to be picked for the netball team. I haven't felt able to get dates when I wanted them. I didn't always feel like I had someone I could discuss important matters with. And I definitely felt ashamed by all of that.

I'm slightly reiterating here what I said in Idea 1: that I didn't realise that I wasn't alone in feeling lonely until I admitted to a friend that I had a problem with loneliness. I really believe that admitting that fact was the first step in overcoming my loneliness. But looking back, the first person that I admitted this to wasn't that friend. It was myself.

I am not an unhappy person. It mightn't come across here, but most of the time I'm really rather contented and optimistic about life. It's just that when I *am* unhappy, the number one source of those feelings of unhappiness is loneliness. Realising that loneliness was the biggest cause of unhappiness in my life, admitting it to *myself* and sticking a label on it, was the first thing that I did towards conquering it.

Admitting it to *another* person, to my friend in the email that I sent (being too cowardly to admit it face-to-face) was the second thing.

But it's not always easy to admit that you're lonely. It's embarrassing for a start. I was worried that telling my friends that I sometimes suffered from feeling lonely could be counter-productive. They might see me as a failure, I might be a "less desirable" friend somehow and then lose the friends that I had. There is such a stigma attached to loneliness – sometimes, I think it would have been easier to say that I had an STD or that I had committed a crime than it was to admit that I felt lonely.

According to author Emily White: "The lonely person, according to conventional wisdom, is to hack through their aloneness by reaching out to someone else and admitting to the problem. The difficulty with this piece of advice is that it doesn't correspond to the reality of loneliness. So much shame and stigma attaches to the state that it's extraordinarily hard to talk about, even in a culture that prides itself on being self-revelatory."

There's so much shame and stigma, in fact, that rather than admitting to my loneliness, for a long time I tried to hide it. I've already mentioned my embarrassment at checking books about loneliness out of the local library. On one occasion, I made a point of actually *saying* to the librarian that I was researching a book because I didn't want her to think I was lonely.

"One of the main problems with loneliness is what I think of as 'visibility'," says Emily White, "the sense of having your loneliness witnessed by others, and of being seen as being too much on your own."

There are so many stereotypes attached to loneliness: people see lonely people as being antisocial, self-obsessed, needy, unattractive or even psychopathic. For instance, the Daily Mail published a photo of the gunman Raoul Moat as a boy, after he'd gone on the rampage in 2010. The caption under the photo read simply: "Loner: as a boy, Moat had few friends."

Admitting my loneliness then, felt like something of a risk. I didn't want anyone to judge me or categorise me as being needy or unattractive as that could end up leaving me lonelier and more isolated than ever before. But it's a catch 22 situation: if you won't admit you're lonely, you can't ask for help. If you admit to feeling lonely, you risk being branded as a loser. "Only losers feel lonely," say psychiatrists Jacqueline Olds and Richard Schwartz. "Only losers don't get picked for the teams, don't have dates when they want them, don't have people with whom they can discuss important matters – so we each keep our loneliness to ourselves, not even wanting to tell therapists about it, and become even more alone in our shame."

So I was very careful about who I told. First the friend in the email – she was someone I knew I could trust and she'd shared her experiences of suffering from anxiety with me already. Encouraged by her positive reaction, I told another friend, Susan (not her real name). She too was suffering from loneliness. I had just never realised.

Suddenly, things snowballed. Susan told me that one of her friends, someone I had met once before, wanted to go on a loneliness retreat. I had seen it advertised too, but didn't want to go on my own in case the other participants thought I was a Billy-No-Mates. I kind of overlooked the fact that they would all be there because *they* felt lonely. I agreed to go on the retreat with Susan's friend, and spent a weekend talking about loneliness to other, very non-judgmental people who were fellow sufferers.

I enjoyed the retreat and wanted to repeat the experience. Soon I found myself saying to Susan's friend and another woman I'd befriended there, "I'm sure *we* could run something like this ourselves." So we did. As the unemployed person in the group, it fell to me to do most of the organising and most of the research. Soon, I was talking about my loneliness easily. I was talking to television executives about loneliness, trying to persuade them to do a documentary (watch this space!) I was talking to publishers about loneliness, trying to persuade them that the self-help literature out there wasn't really up to the mark. I was talking to retreat centres about putting on more retreats about loneliness.

I don't always get a positive response. I once told someone at a church meeting that I was running a retreat on loneliness and writing a book about it. She asked why and I explained that I sometimes struggled with feelings of loneliness myself. I later overheard her gossiping about me to someone else and they ignored me socially for the rest of the day. I resolved to exercise a little more caution about who I told in the future.

Despite this, admitting I felt lonely was one of the best things that I ever did. If I hadn't done it, I think I'd probably still be sitting on the sofa watching *Come Dine with Me* all weekend and feeling thoroughly miserable that I had nothing else to do.

Perhaps I'll never be completely free of loneliness. Perhaps loneliness will strike whenever my life circumstances change, whenever a relationship breaks down, I lose my job or I have to move to a new place. Or perhaps it will simply strike when it feels like, when there's no reason other than not having enough to do, the cold weather of a British winter or the dark December nights.

But right now, I'm hardly watching TV and I'm spending my time doing other things that leave me feeling more satisfied and contented.

Likewise, I've gone from someone who turned to Facebook, Match.com and Hotmail whenever she was feeling bored, to someone who *usually* turns to creative things like writing a journal or writing letters. Far more fulfilling!

I'm arranging things with my "A list" friends first before my diary gets crowded out with other social commitments because it's those deep and meaningful conversations with my closest friends that make me feel most connected.

I've gone from being the girl who was nick-named "Weed of the week" by her PE teacher at school because she was so useless at sport to being someone who runs every day (though I didn't fit it in whilst writing this book!) and who is running a 10K for charity in the summer.

I've gone from being someone who didn't feel she quite fitted in as a child to someone who has lots of good friends and who accepts that she simply doesn't always like what other people like: I prefer going to bed with a good book to partying all night.

I'm learning to like being alone. I don't always manage it, but most of the time, I do. I have things that I love doing and when I find myself alone, I try to get on with them.

I've gone from being someone who didn't feel that she could talk about feeling lonely, to someone who's very much at ease sharing her feelings of loneliness. I run retreats about loneliness and I'm hoping to start work on that documentary later in the year.

I've gone from someone who was *desperate* to meet the right man to someone who has let go of that need. I would still like to meet him. But it's no longer the be all and end all of my life. I'm trying not to allow that expectation that I *should* be married and settled down by the age of 42 to make me feel lonely any more.

I've gone from being bored with my life to having lots of interests and projects that keep me going, even during those periods of unemployment. My Help100 project, in which I'm trying to help 100 people in a life-changing way, is one of those projects and I'll be using all the proceeds from this book for that (see www.Help100.org.uk for further details).

And I've gone from being someone with a bookcase full of chick-lit and romantic novels to someone whose shelves heave under the weight of self-help, psychology and "mind, body, spirit" books, with the occasional theological textbook thrown in for good measure. But right now, I want to stop reading *about* loneliness and start enjoying life without it.

Finally, I'd like to wish you good luck with your quest to find freedom from loneliness. It is possible. With a little perseverance.

For further information, please visit my website
All-The-Lonely-People.org.uk

Selected Bibliography

10 Days to Great Self-esteem by Dr. David Burns

15 days of Prayer with Henri Nouwen by Robert Waldron

A Book of Silence by Sara Maitland

A Good Talk by Daniel Menaker

Alone Together by Sherry Turkle

An Unknown Woman by Alice Koller

Be the Person You Want to Find by Cheri Huber

Becoming Who You Are by James Martin

Beyond Singleness by Helena Wilkinson

Bowling Alone by Robert Putnam

Breaking Free from Loneliness by Helena Wilkinson

Building Self-esteem by Sue Atkinson

Celebrating Time Alone: Stories of Splendid Solitude by Lionel Fisher

Change Your Life in 7 Days by Paul McKenna

Connected: The Amazing Power of Social Networks and How They Shape Our Lives by Nicholas Christakis and James Fowler

Crossing by Mark Barrett

Eat Pray Love by Elizabeth Gilbert

Everything I've Ever Done That Worked by Lesley Garner

Finding Happiness by Christopher Jamison

Growing Into Silence by Paul Nicholson

How to Be Happy by Liz Goddard

How To Get From Where You Are To Where You Want To Be by Cheri Huber

How to Raise Your Self-esteem by Nathaniel Branden

How to Talk To Anyone by Leil Lowndes

In Praise of Slow by Carl Honoré

Live Alone and Like it by Marjorie Hillis

Loneliness: Human Nature and the Need for Social Connection by John Cacioppo

Loneliness: The Experience of Emotional and Social Isolation by Robert Weiss

Lonely: A Memoir by Emily White

Man's Search for Meaning by Viktor Frankl

Managing Your Mind: The Mental Fitness Guide by Gillian Butler and Tony Hope

Overcoming Loneliness in Everyday Life by Jacqueline Olds, Richard Schwartz and Harriet Webster

Positive Solitude by Rae Andre

Reaching Out by Henri Nouwen

Shortcuts to Bouncing Back from Heartbreak by Gael Lindenfeld

Single and Loving It by Wendy Bristow

Singled Out by Virginia Nicholson

Solace: The Missing Dimension in Psychiatry by Dr Paul Horton

Solitude by Anthony Storr

Staying Sane by Dr. Raj Persaud

Succulent Wild Woman by Sark

The Art of Happiness by the Dalai Lama and Howard C. Cutler

The Artists Way by Julia Cameron

The Feeling Good Handbook by Dr. David Burns

The Happiness Project by Gretchen Rubin

The Lonely American by Jacqueline Olds and Richard Schwartz

The Lonely Screams by Sean S. Seepersad

The Lonely Society by the Mental Health Foundation

The Loss of Happiness in Market Democracies by Robert E Lane

The Miracle of Mindfulness by Thich Nhat Hanh

The Stations of Solitude by Alice Koller

There Is Nothing Wrong With You by Cheri Huber

Travelling Light by Daniel O'Leary

Walden by Henry David Thoreau

19617849R00131

Made in the USA
Lexington, KY
30 December 2012